S0-BAQ-904

A Guide to the Gamelan

A Guide to the Gamelan

Neil Sorrell

Amadeus
Press

\# 22928402

ML
3758
.J3
S67
1990

First published in 1990
by Faber and Faber Limited
3 Queen Square London WC1N 3AU

Photoset by Parker Typesetting Service Leicester
Printed in Great Britain by
Clays Ltd, St Ives plc

All rights reserved

© Neil Sorrell, 1990

Neil Sorrell is hereby identified as author
of this work in accordance with Section 77 of the
Copyrights, Designs and Patents Act 1988.

*This book is sold subject to the condition that it shall
not, by way of trade or otherwise, be lent, resold,
hired out or otherwise circulated without the
publisher's prior consent in any form of binding or
cover other than that in which it is published and
without a similar condition including this condition
being imposed on the subsequent purchaser.*

A CIP record for this book is
available from the British Library

ISBN 0–571–14401–2
ISBN 0–571–14404–7 (paperback)

First published in North America in 1990 by
Amadeus Press (an imprint of Timber Press, Inc.)
9999 S.W. Wilshire
Portland, Oregon 97225, U.S.A.

ISBN 0–931340–33–0 (cloth)
ISBN 0–931340–34–9 (paper)

Contents

HOLY SPIRIT LIBRARY
92 2159
CABRINI COLLEGE, RADNOR, PA.

Preface

Be not afeard. The isle is full of noises,
Sounds, and sweet airs, that give delight, and hurt not.
Sometimes a thousand twangling instruments
Will hum about mine ears; and sometime voices,
That, if I then had wak'd after long sleep,
Will make me sleep again; and then, in dreaming,
The clouds methought would open and show riches
Ready to drop upon me, that, when I wak'd,
I cried to dream again.

What better way to begin a study of Javanese gamelan music from an English perspective than with lines of our greatest poet? The speech of Caliban in Act 3 scene ii of Shakespeare's *The Tempest*, describing Prospero's magic island, has the universality and truth of poetic beauty to convey the essence of Java and its music better than any scholarly prose or the efforts of this book.* We must first try to capture the poetic inspiration and then to explain. As performers of gamelan music and audiences increase, so it becomes more important to have a means of understanding the sounds at a basic level. Books on the subject (in English) have tended to be either lengthy and specialized or else brief introductions avoiding detailed discussion of the music. Students, teachers, and the musical public require an introduction which gives the context of gamelan music and an insight into its workings. Over the past ten years or so I have been asked to give introductory lectures and

---

* I was reminded of these wonderful lines by Alec Roth, who used the first four of them to introduce performances of his exquisite settings, for voices and gamelan, of two of Ariel's songs from this play.

workshops in gamelan playing. From the kinds of materials, explanations, and questions arising, not to mention constant requests for further reading, came the main impetus behind this book. It provides a grounding in the subject, from which the interested reader may continue to the longer, more specialized works, which generally assume this prior knowledge. For those who have never played gamelan it may whet their appetite to try, on one of the many sets now available!

The sight of a gamelan laid out in all its beauty provides the best definition of the word, a generic term for widely differing ensembles, comprising predominantly percussion instruments, usually made of bronze and mounted on intricately carved wooden frames. Most gamelans come from the Indonesian islands of Java and Bali, and an introduction to all the different kinds of gamelan, on equal terms, would stretch the length of this book and the expertise of its author beyond reasonable limits. Instead, the study is confined to the typical Central Javanese gamelan, and specifically the tradition in the city of Solo (Surakarta), which is not only one of the most important in Indonesia, but has also become the main gamelan type outside.

Because the justification for this book is not simply the mechanics of the gamelan and its music but how and why it has made such an impact in the West, the first chapter examines the phenomenon, especially with reference to composers and music educators. From a brief general introduction to the historical, geographical and cultural context in Java, the book proceeds to an examination of the instruments of the Central Javanese gamelan, including some information on the fascinating subject of how they are made. The following chapter, on the subject of *karawitan* – the traditional music of the Javanese gamelan – arms the reader with the rudiments and terminology of the 'software'. The application of this musical system to the instruments of the gamelan is described in the final chapter, in which a piece is analysed to illustrate what may be considered typical in gamelan music. The concluding summary returns to the theme of what all this means to us.

Acknowledgements

This book is dedicated to Gamelan Sekar Pethak, to its makers and to all who have played on it or will do so. It must be unusual to dedicate a book to a set of musical instruments, but the gamelan, in keeping with Javanese beliefs, is not to be dismissed as a collection of inanimate objects.

The dedication is also an attempt to include most of the people to whom special thanks are due: first and foremost to the maker of the gamelan, Tentrem Sarwanto, and his team of craftsmen; Hadi Adnan in Jakarta, Suparmin Sunjoyo in London, and Tony Sunaryo in Yogyakarta, for their help with packing and freighting the instruments; the English Gamelan Orchestra (who helped inaugurate Gamelan Sekar Pethak in York on 30 April 1982); the students of the York University music department, who stuck their necks out in the first place by coming to the department, and further by joining the gamelan group (much of the book grew out of the stimulus of working with them); to my Javanese teachers, who either helped inaugurate Gamelan Sekar Pethak in Java, on 22 November 1981, or else have played and taught on it in England, including I. M. Harjito, A. L. Sutikno, Sri Hastanto, Rahayu Supanggah, A. L. Suwardi, Supardi, Sukamso, Panggiyo, and especially Joko Purwanto (who demonstrates some of the instruments in the photographs).

The dedication also includes distinguished visitors to York who worked with us: Lou Harrison and William Colvig, who brought their creative skills from California and gave us new perspectives on gamelan and its music, and His Excellency Bapak Suhartoyo, who gave of his valuable time and expertise to introduce us to the pinnacle of his country's culture, *wayang kulit* (shadow play). Some names slip through this net: most important are my first gamelan teacher (1969–71), the late Prawotosaputro, and his assistants at Wesleyan University (USA), especially Shitalakshmi Prawirohardjo, and Bob Brown, a driving force behind gamelan studies in those years. The present director of the gamelan at Wesleyan, Sumarsam, shared his very interesting and original theories with me during my most recent visit to Wesleyan (Fall Semester 1989), principally to study with him and, once more, with I. M. Harjito. Without the guidance of these two excellent teachers and musicians this book may still have been possible, but it would have been virtually devoid of that essential ingredient: the Javanese perspective. There can hardly be a page that does not owe some debt to the inspiration of Harjito and Sumarsam. Any mistakes and misconceptions must be the product of my own Western – hence relatively inexperienced – mind.

Finally, thanks are due to Donald Mitchell for his kindness in reading the manuscript, the wisdom of his suggestions, and the benefit of his influence, and to certain graduates of the York music department: Peter Murphy and Liz Haddon, for their help and encouragement with the more tedious business of reading, correcting, copying and typing; and Maria Mendonca for our valuable discussions. A special debt of gratitude is due to Ben Arps, who, at very short notice and with much more urgent things to do, read the entire manuscript and sent almost as thick a sheaf of comments and corrections. His expertise is welcome not only to me but to the whole gamelan community in England. Noémie Mendelle was a dear companion and excellent critic throughout the unduly long period of writing, and I think it is no paradox that her lack of musical training gave me perhaps my clearest insight into the power and value of the gamelan.

Spelling and Pronunciation

The official language of the Republic of Indonesia, of which Java is the most populous island, is Indonesian (*Bahasa Indonesia*), but a great number of regional languages (*bahasa daerah*) are spoken throughout the islands and more than one in Java itself. The terminology used in this book is a combination of Indonesian and Javanese (the main regional language of Central and Eastern Java), which results in certain conflicts of spelling and pronunciation. A good example is the pronunciation of the letter 'a', which the Javanese often pronounce more like an 'o', especially in final and dependent penultimate open syllables. Thus words like *sanga*, *gangsa* and *gatra* will be pronounced by the Javanese more like 'songo', 'gongso' and 'gotro'. Conversely, the town of Solo is rarely written as Sala, while Surabaya is hardly ever written as Suroboyo.

Further confusion arises from the fact that in 1972 the Indonesian government adopted a different orthography for the language. For English speakers it represents a simplification and general improvement, with perhaps the exception of 'th' for the retroflex 't' (adopted from Javanese orthography in 1974). For example, the word *patet* is now written *pathet*, but of course the pronunciation has not changed, and 'th' should never be pronounced as in English. The modern orthography has been adopted in this book (though without diacritical marks, which are given in the glossary (p.127–35)).

The simplest approach to pronunciation is to use the approximate Received Standard English equivalents (avoiding diphthongs), with the following qualifications and exceptions:

Vowels

a   see above
e   as in mom*e*nt
è   as in mom*e*ntum
é   as in m*a*te
u   variously as in tr*u*th or p*u*t, never as in b*u*t

Consonants

c   as in *ch*ip
dh   'd' with the tongue slightly further back
g   as in *g*et, rather than *g*entle (thus, the instrument named *gender* should never be pronounced like the English word denoting the distinction between the sexes)
k   glottal stop at the end of a word or syllable
–ng– as in ha*ng*er
–ngg– as in a*ng*er
r   rolled
th   't' with the tongue slightly further back (*not* as in *th*e or *th*ing)

It is not usual to mark plurals with the final letter 's', but in spoken English it is quite normal to use it with Javanese and Indonesian words, especially the more common ones (one gamelan, two gamelans, etc.) and this liberty has been taken in this book, with the reminder that such plural forms are English modifications of foreign words.

Notation

Gamelan music is essentially an oral (or aural) tradition, but in the last hundred years various notations have been devised, firstly as a means of preserving compositions and now as part of the teaching process. The only system in common use, and certainly one of the simplest notations in the world, is the *kepatihan* cipher system.

Each note in the scale is given a number. A rest, or a prolongation of a note, is indicated by a dot or dash. Sequences of notes, rests, or both, are grouped into fours (each called a *gatra*) and spaced off from each other for ease of legibility.

The upper octave of a note is indicated by a dot above the number, and the lower octave by a dot below.

A line across two or more notes indicates that their length is halved; thus $\overline{12}$ $\overline{35}$ or $\overline{1235}$ move at twice the speed of 1 2 3 5. Similarly, the rhythm   a/w   would be shown in this notation as $\overline{\overline{1-2}}$ $\overline{\overline{3-5}}$ (assuming a pulse equivalent to a crotchet).

Certain instruments have special symbols. Although these are not completely standardized, the ones employed in this book may be considered to be as prevalent as any others.

rebab (two-stringed fiddle)

\	down bow
/	up bow
a b c d	fingering (1st, 2nd, 3rd, 4th)
I II III etc.	position

kendhang (drums)

symbol	sound (onomatopoeic)	played
o	*tong*	left hand: one or two fingers at the edge
+	*tak*	left hand: gentle slap with all fingers near the middle
|	*ket*	right hand: tap with one finger near the middle
p	*dhung*	right hand: bounced stroke with one or all fingers near the middle
b	*bem/dhah*	right hand: bounced stroke with all fingers near the edge

These are only some of the sounds. The more elaborate repertoire for the *ciblon* drum is excluded because it is not notated in this book. When a combination of two drums is used (*kendhang II*) the first four sounds (o, +, | and p) are played on the smaller drum, and only *bem* (b) on the larger. In the modified staff notation used in Chapter 5 (see below), the first four sounds are placed on the upper monotone (representing the smaller drum) and the last (b) on the lower monotone (representing the larger drum). Left-hand strokes are notated with stems down and right-hand strokes with stems up.

Colotomic (punctuating) instruments (gongs):

symbol	instrument
×	*kethuk*
o	*kempyang*
∧	*kenong*
∨	*kempul*
( )	gong (*ageng* or *suwukan*)

In the Javanese cipher system, notations for certain instruments played with two mallets simultaneously (this applies especially to the *gender*s) separate the hands by a horizontal line: —

$$\frac{\text{right hand}}{\text{left hand}}$$

– which may be continuous or intermittent, according to the instrument. Notations for the *bonangs* (gong-chimes), which are also played with two mallets, but usually consecutively rather than simultaneously, do not normally use this line, and consequently do not indicate which hand should play which note.

Modified staff notation

This was devised by the author specially for the extended transcription at the end of Chapter 5 of this book, in order to help those who may prefer a more graphic and familiar notation to the Javanese cipher system. It is impossible to notate gamelan pitches accurately on a conventional stave with clefs. The first modification, therefore, is to dispense with Western clefs and to substitute a Javanese equivalent: S for *slendro* (the tuning system of the piece concerned) and P for *pelog* (the other tuning system of the gamelan). The five approximately equidistant pitches of the typical *slendro* tuning then fit conveniently on to the five lines for the middle octave (with upper and lower octaves being placed on ledger lines above or below the stave). *Pelog* can be adapted to the stave, with smaller gaps between its seven pitches, compared to the five of *slendro*:

Each stave represents the medium octave for the instrument concerned (the relative registers are explained in the written account of the instruments). Monotones are used for the *kendhang* (drums), since definite pitches are not usually heard, and also for the *gong ageng*, of which the pitch is neither standardized nor easily notated.

Another advantage of this system is that it permits the use of the normal Western rhythmic notation. The pulse of the *balungan* (the skeletal melody of the composition) is here taken to be a minim, and metronome marks can be used to indicate the kinds of tempi which would be typical in performance. Barlines, which could be very misleading, are avoided. Rests, shown in the Javanese cipher system by dots or dashes (in place of the numbers), do not necessarily mean a complete cessation of the sound. It depends on the technique of the instrument concerned and the general context. For the sake of consistency such dots and dashes are always shown as rests in the modified staff notation, with the reminder that in performance they are just as likely to be treated as ties. This applies especially to the *rebab* (bowed instrument) which sustains an almost unbroken sound throughout.

To facilitate comparison, both notational systems are used, the Javanese cipher equivalent under the modified staff notation. Staff notation obviously 'Westernizes' the music to some extent, but the aim of this book is precisely to make gamelan music comprehensible and relevant to Westerners who are unfamiliar with it, and therefore the compromise seems justified. It must be emphasized that the above system was developed only for limited use within this book, and the best rule to observe with gamelan music in performance is that, since all notations are new-fangled and unsatisfactory, the less they are used, the better.

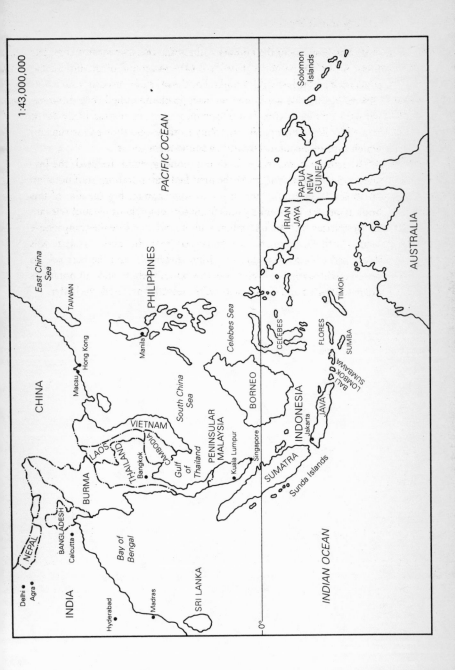

1:43,000,000

xvii

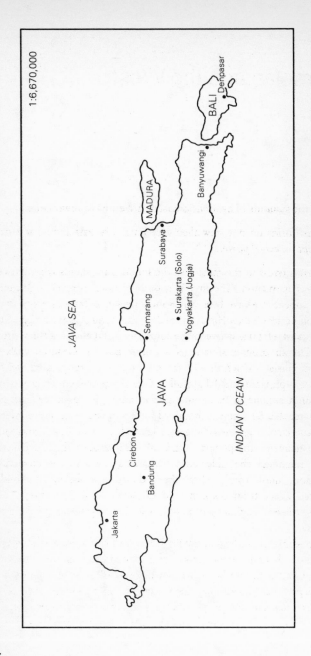

1:6,670,000

JAVA SEA

JAVA

INDIAN OCEAN

Jakarta

Bandung

Cirebon

Semarang

Surakarta (Solo)

Yogyakarta (Jogja)

Surabaya

MADURA

Banyuwangi

BALI

Denpasar

Chapter 1

Gamelan and the West

'On the summits of awareness East and West have always met.'

'Alien forms do not stay alien very long. *The exotic does not exist except on travel posters.*'[1]

Western interest in the musics of the Indonesian islands is a relatively recent phenomenon. The first European of note to react to Javanese music appears to have been Sir Francis Drake. A famous entry in the logbook of the *Golden Hind* (1580) describes a musical exchange on the south coast of Java between the local ruler and the English visitors: 'Raia Donan coming aboard us ... presented our Generall with his country musick, which though it were of a very strange kind, yet the sound was pleasant and delightfull.'[2] After this passing reference, which we cannot assume to be about gamelan music, it was more than 200 years later that Sir Thomas Stamford Raffles took a more active interest in Javanese culture, researching the island's history and importing gamelan instruments and puppets into England. It appears that these instruments remained the only ones here, and, even so, in unplayable condition, until 1977, when the Indonesian embassy in London acquired a set from Solo, named Gamelan Kyai Rawatmeja. This marked the real beginning of practical studies of gamelan music in this country.

Jaap Kunst[3] remarks that the English were always pioneers of interest and research in Javanese music, and especially so in the nineteenth century, but it should be noted that these scholars were not primarily musicians. Foremost among them was A. J. Ellis, whose study of the Javanese *slendro* and *pelog* tunings and other non-European scales, presented in his famous paper of 1885,[4] led directly to the creation of ethnomusicology as a scholarly discipline. As so often happens, it was the musicians themselves who were the last to recognize the worth of an alien culture, though it must be said that the dawn, when it broke, was magnificent.

The year 1889, the centenary of the French Revolution, was marked by a Grand Universal Exhibition in Paris, and there, on the Champ de Mars where the Eiffel Tower was erected, Claude Debussy attended performances by Javanese gamelan players and dancers. In 1887 van Vleuten, Minister of the Interior for the Dutch East Indies, had presented the Paris Conservatoire with a gamelan, consisting of sixteen instruments in the *slendro* tuning. It had come from a court in Cirebon, West Java (as distinct from the larger Central Javanese gamelan discussed in this book) and in 1933 it was moved to the Musée de l'Homme, where it remains on display and is used for classes. Thus it is possible that Debussy had already familiarized himself with at least the (*slendro*) scale of these instruments before the 1889 exhibition.[5] His enthusiastic reactions to that event are well documented and are still among the most interesting, perceptive – even prophetic – writings on gamelan music. In fact, they are the key to the understanding of the relevance of gamelan music to Western composition, and Debussy was the first great composer to demonstrate this interest. His most famous writing on the subject came late in his career, in 1913, long after witnessing the Javanese performances, but this is surely proof of the lasting impression they had made. Writing in the *Revue S.I.M.* with characteristic enthusiasm and sarcasm, he made the following claims:

> There were, and there still are, despite the evils of civilization, some delightful native peoples for whom music is as natural as breathing. Their conservatoire is the eternal rhythm of the sea, the wind among the leaves and the thousand sounds of nature which they understand without consulting an arbitrary treatise. Their traditions reside in old songs, combined with dances, built up throughout the centuries. Yet Javanese music is based on a type of counterpoint by comparison with which that of Palestrina is child's play. And if we listen without European prejudice to the charm of their percussion we must confess that our percussion is like primitive noises at a country fair.[6]

Allowing for translation this description echoes Caliban's speech with which I began, as well as reading like a list of pieces by Debussy himself!

It is Debussy the nature-worshipper, the anti-academic, the musician whose struggle to escape from the Teutonic stranglehold and European ethnocentricity in general could have led him just as easily to sign himself *'musicien mondial'* as *'musicien français'*. Overlooking, for the moment, the rather invidious comparison with Palestrina, we come to the wonderful phrase 'the charm of their percussion' (which could be the title for this book) and the perfectly fair comparison with Western percussion. One achievement of twentieth-century music has been the emancipation of percussion – the realization of possibilities far beyond the military pomp and special effects of the deservedly-named 'kitchen department'. Simply put, 'charm' is no longer an incongruous word to apply to percussion. In certain cases one could even talk of the 'gamelanization' of the symphony orchestra; from the turn of this century, if not before, composers as distinct in aesthetic aspiration as Debussy, Stravinsky and Mahler have recognized – and capitalized upon – the myriad of subtle, evocative timbres that can be conjured, gamelan-like, from the extended percussion section of a symphony orchestra.

It would be incorrect to suggest that the whole impetus behind this exploration of percussion came from the gamelan, though in many cases this is undoubtedly so, and there is evidence of actual imitation. It is with Debussy, however, that we come to the crux of the argument. The assumption is that, because Debussy fell in love with gamelan music, he felt compelled to consummate the discovery by imitating it in his own compositions. If he ever did anything so obvious and naive it would be most likely in immature pieces of his post-Rome, post-Bayreuth period of exploration and experimentation.[7] It is pointless to go through the famous music of his maturity looking for traces of gamelan like the fossilized footprints of some rare animal. The better the fusion, the less identifiable the constituents. The greater the composer the less likely such marks are to show, for the simple reason that they have been completely assimilated within the style. It could be argued that Debussy's best music shows no influence of Javanese gamelan at all. The key word is *influence*, with its suggestion of bringing about a change of course. With Debussy a much more fruitful word would be *confirmation*. It seems far more plausible that what he heard in 1889 confirmed what he had, at least subconsciously, always felt about music, and this experience went far deeper than a desire to imitate something new and exotic. The brittle textures of the String Quartet's second movement,

3

often cited as a possible instance of gamelan-inspired writing, are hardly typical of the mellifluous resonances of the Javanese gamelan, and there is no point in trying to link it with the familiar Balinese gamelan *gong kebyar*, which had not yet been invented. It is not until more than a decade later, the period of Debussy's most mature and personal style, and the masterpieces of the twentieth-century such as *La Mer* and the *Estampes*, that characteristics possibly associated with gamelan music become really interesting, if only because the ideas are more assimilated and subtle. It is also worth noting that Spanish *influence* plays a far greater role, if only because it is overt. Even here, though, it is not a matter of imitation or souvenirs (since Debussy barely set foot in Spain) but rather the product of a remarkable imagination.

Should we therefore conclude that the contact with gamelan music is easily overestimated as far as Debussy's actual music is concerned? Although the appearance of some pages of *La Mer*,[8] with their instrumental stratification, isorhythms and multiple ostinati, look like 'gamelan music', (perhaps a paradoxical phrase) there is little in his output which actually sounds like it. This emphasis on looking rather than sounding like gamelan music could be significant, as Debussy's interest in gamelan music may have been almost as much in its transcribed appearance as in its actual sound. The stratification and polyphony of ostinati in gamelan music are abundantly obvious in attempts to represent the music in Western staff notation.[9]

Whether or not Debussy would have been content to study an abstract notation without recourse to the actual timbres, which such a notation is incapable of conveying, is another matter. He did not use the *pelog* scale (with which he seems to have been unfamiliar) and the supposed nearest Western equivalent to *slendro* (the 'black-note', or pentatonic scale) is so common in Europe and throughout the world that its frequent occurrence in Debussy's music cannot be attributed solely to Javanese sources. The pentatonic scales, ostinati and percussive sonorities in Debussy's music (as well as in the works of many of his influential predecessors, from Wagner and Liszt to Mussorgsky) are as likely to have been inspired by the local church bells as anything further afield, in which case the experience of the gamelan was essentially a confirmation of the connection. Nor did Debussy embark on an extensive and radical use of percussion, in the manner of Varèse or Cage, though he did exploit that quality of charm which he so admired in the gamelan. The earlier distinction between influence (or imitation), and confirmation (or reinforcement) can also be expressed in terms of parallels rather than convergences. To talk about numerous parallels between Debussy's work and gamelan music is more rewarding, and again we can turn to his writings for support. On the subject of his self-confessed religion, which was Nature, he claimed that music is not concerned with reproducing nature, but instead with the mysterious affinity ('concordances') between Nature and the imagination. Thus music does not converge with nature in some sort of crude imitation, but parallels it in a deeper, mysterious way.

The nearest parallel to the *slendro* scale in Debussy is not, after all, the 'black-note' pentatonic scale (which is perhaps the nearest imitation, if one were to be sought) but the whole-tone hexatonic scale. This is not only because it is an equidistant scale but also because it disrupts the tonic–dominant polarity of the diatonic scale. Debussy's other famous remark on gamelan music was in a letter to Pierre Louÿs in 1895, in which he wrote: 'Do you not remember the Javanese music, able to express every shade of meaning, even unmentionable shades and which makes our tonic and dominant seem like ghosts?'[10]

If the Javanese achieve this partly with their *slendro* scale, and Debussy partly with his whole-tone scale, the effect in both cases is to show a new musical domain beyond the constraints of Western classical tonality. Non-Western music offers the possibility of maintaining some sort of tonality without putting the clock back to the nineteenth century. It is also arguable that this modality led to a freer use of sonority, and here Debussy's revolution was perhaps at its most striking. Many of his piano pieces of the first decade of this century may remind the listener of gamelan music through the richness, subtlety and resonance of their sonorities. (Only one, incidentally, has a title suggesting an unmistakably oriental origin, and that is 'Pagodes', the first of the *Estampes*. Yet that is hardly as explicitly Javanese as, for example, 'Soirée dans Grenade' is explicitly Spanish; quite apart from anything else, Java is not a land of pagodas.) In order to achieve these unique sonorities Debussy required that the piano should sound as if it had no hammers. In this respect the parallel with Javanese gamelan is quite remarkable, because in its fullest and most sophisticated version that ensemble sounds as if it is played without mallets, and, indeed, instruments of the *gender* family most closely attain Debussy's ideal (even if

5

he may, ironically, have been unfamiliar with them). Furthermore, both the gamelan and Debussy's piano release an extremely rich pattern of overtones. In a Javanese *pendhapa* (pavilion) one can hear this additional layer of music as if it were floating in the roof. (Perhaps it is this 'uncomposed' acoustical complexity that really warrants the comparison with Palestrina.) It could even be suggested that the timbre of the flute, viola and harp combination (in the second of the three late sonatas) parallels that of the *suling*, *rebab* and *celempung* or *kacapi* (flute, fiddle, and plucked zither, respectively) instruments of Java, though there is no evidence that Debussy had any conscious desire to make such a connection.

Another interesting conjecture has arisen in occasional seminars on Debussy's music in which various works were mentioned for their affinities with gamelan music. Apart from the much-cited *La Mer*, they were 'Reflets dans l'eau', 'Ondine', and 'Sirènes'. Lockspeiser has written of the pervasive influence of water in Debussy's music,[11] and commentators on gamelan music use aquatic imagery to try and describe the fluid sonorities of the gamelan which manage to convey the impression of stasis and movement at the same time, like a flowing stream.

The question arising from all these opinions is: what would a Javanese musician make of Debussy's allegedly gamelan-inspired pieces? The most recent of these seminars was held in the University of York in May 1989, to mark the centenary of Debussy's encounter with the Javanese music at the Paris Exhibition. Paul Roberts, a pianist specializing in Debussy, presided, and we were fortunate to have Joko Purwanto, an expert gamelan player, in residence as a graduate student. After a selection of piano pieces by Debussy he was asked if he was struck by any similarities with gamelan music. His reply was most revealing and touched on the real problem. What to others may have sounded Javanese sounded to him more vaguely south-east Asian, from Cambodia for example (so, by a fortunate coincidence, he was associating the music with a real area of pagodas). The overriding factor which prevents such music from sounding Javanese to a Javanese is the tuning. Gamelan music is in *pelog* or *slendro*, and no matter how evocative the piece, the piano cannot reproduce these tunings. This may help discourage the confusion of general orientalisms in Western music with specifically Javanese gamelan elements.

Further research is obviously necessary before the degree of Debussy's knowledge of the gamelan, one of the most exciting and discussed topics in the history of twentieth-century Western music, is understood. The points raised here cannot profess to be the last word on the subject, but a few interim conclusions may be offered. The more the written accounts of the 1889 exhibition are considered, including the attempts at notating the Javanese music, the more doubts are raised about what exactly Debussy heard there. It is highly likely that, while it was broadly similar to the music of the full Central Javanese gamelan discussed in this book, it was significantly different in detail. We must remember that we are not only dealing with an historical gap of 100 years but also a wide geographical and stylistic distribution of music within Java, which could well have been reflected at the Exhibition without any European being aware of it. If Debussy tried out the Cirebon instruments donated to the Paris Conservatoire, he would not have found all the instruments of the Central Javanese gamelan among them. Nor is it established that he heard a complete Central Javanese set at the 1889 exhibition either. We know that the musicians and dancers came from the Central Javanese courts, and so the assumption is that they played their usual instruments. It was, and still is, however, common practice for visiting troupes to save money and trouble by borrowing instruments which are already in the country they are visiting. It is possible, therefore, that Debussy heard the reduced instrumentarium of the Cirebon set, and virtually certain that he only heard the *slendro* tuning.

Though Debussy undoubtedly raised the level of Western consciousness apropos the music of the East, if one wishes to find examples of music more overtly inspired by the gamelan it is easier to look at works of later composers. The dramatic increase in performance and recordings of non-Western music in Europe and America, accompanied by scholarly investigations, has ensured the wider dissemination and absorption of these exotic sources. Messiaen's music is perhaps no less subtle and elusive than Debussy's, yet the difference is that Messiaen is at pains to reveal the sources of his art. When he uses an Indian rhythm he tells us, even in the score itself, and in a work like the gigantic *Turangalîla-Symphonie* he even refers to part of the sizeable percussion section as a 'gamelang'. In fact, by the late 1940s, when the Symphony was written, Messiaen was scarcely better placed than Debussy for access to oriental music. Like Debussy, he did not need more than samples; his imagination and inspiration did the rest.

There have been many fine attempts, by composers such as Percy Grainger, Godowsky and Colin McPhee, to realize the inspiration of gamelan music in terms of Western music; but probably the most obvious and successful imitation is in Benjamin Britten's ballet *The Prince of the Pagodas* (ironically, one of the composer's least admired works). There is no doubt that Britten wanted to imitate the (Balinese) gamelan for a special effect, and the result, using a more or less standard symphony orchestra, is so successful that one is almost deceived into thinking that it really *is* a gamelan. The fascinating story behind the ballet, of Britten's contacts with Balinese music and his trip to Bali, is well documented. Perhaps his most famous remark, which nicely balances Debussy's comparison between the (Javanese) gamelan and Palestrina, was: 'The music is fantastically rich – melodically, rhythmically, texture (such orchestration!) and above all formally. It's a remarkable culture ... at last I'm beginning to catch on to the technique, but it's about as complicated as Schönberg'.[12]

Britten was introduced to Balinese music during his stay in America (1939–42) by the Canadian composer and expert on the subject, Colin McPhee (with whom he played transcriptions of Balinese music at the piano). In 1952 John Coast brought a group from the Balinese village of Pliatan to Europe and America. Prior to the tour, he devised a programme with them in Bali, during which he played a recording of Britten's *Young Person's Guide to the Orchestra* and asked for a similar Balinese piece. *Kapi Raja* (a piece in the North Balinese *kebyar* style) was suggested. It appears that Britten came across this piece, possibly unaware of the part he had played in it, on a record of the 1952 visit by the Pliatan gamelan to England. We do not know that he attended the actual performances in London, or that he read John Coast's account of the origin of *Kapi Raja* (and the sleeve notes of the recording make no mention of the Britten connection), or that he even visited Pliatan during his visit to Bali in 1956. (The nearest we come is a reference to 'near Ubud' in his sketches, which could well mean Pliatan, since the two villages are virtually connected.) It seems, therefore, a wonderful coincidence that Britten came across *Kapi Raja*, which he used, along with sketches from Bali, in *The Prince of the Pagodas*. Yet there would be nothing of profound importance if his involvement with gamelan music rested solely on this work. The point about Britten, as with Debussy, is that the contact reinforced the composer's pre-existing beliefs. Donald Mitchell's important insight concerning Britten is virtually the same point I have tried to make concerning Debussy (or any other prominent composer who is concerned with more than exotic opportunities for imitation):

> ... the experience of Bali was not so much the moment of ignition (though of course the impact of the trip was profound) but, rather, the *living confirmation* [my italics] of what Britten already had in mind.[13]

Thus, for Britten, the techniques found in gamelan music were far more important than the brief, yet highly successful, imitation in *The Prince of the Pagodas*. Indeed, he became interested in heterophonic textures before he even became acquainted with gamelan music. Somsak Ketukaenchan has drawn attention to the heterophony in the early operetta *Paul Bunyan* (1941) at the words 'Look at the moon! It's turning blue'; and connections with gamelan are evident almost throughout Britten's entire output, from *Paul Bunyan*, through *Owen Wingrave* (1970), to his last opera, *Death in Venice* (1973).[14]

Although the discussion has dwelt so far on European composers, the greatest interest in gamelan music has come from outside Europe, mainly in America but also in Australia, New Zealand and Japan. There is an obvious reason for this. Even to a thoroughly European composer such as Debussy the experience of non-Western music was, as I have said, one antidote to the all-pervasive Germanic symphonic tradition, and to the influence especially of Wagner. Several American and Antipodean composers, despite a natural inclination to maintain their European connection, began to explore the musics of lands that are actually nearer to them than Europe.

The Californian perspective, expressed by Bertram Turetzky, is typical of this shift of emphasis:

> I think that the point is that I and many other Americans are more interested in what is going on in the East than in looking to Mother Europe for a nod of acceptance. By Mother Europe I mean basically Germany, Italy and France – the nations with the monopoly of so many aspects of music for so many years. So many Americans still look to Europe for answers and guidance and I felt that just isn't the answer. It is not a question of disrespect – it's a question of a man having to find his own sound world in an aesthetic and artistic sense.[15]

9

Drawing once again on Debussy's shrewd and prophetic observations, his comparison with Palestrina should warn against exaggerating the affinity between gamelan music and so-called Minimal music, lest the implication arise that gamelan music is itself in some way minimal. True, Steve Reich studied Balinese gamelan but the real impetus for his process pieces came from experiments with tape loops, and whatever parallels he sought in gamelan music for this kind of mechanical heterophony were found later. On the inspiration of non-Western music, Reich's position is fundamentally the same as that of the great composers already discussed:

> The least interesting form of influence, to my mind, is that of imitating the *sound* of some non-Western music.
>
> Alternately; one can create a music with one's own sound that is constructed in the light of one's knowledge of non-Western *structures*.
>
> This brings about the interesting situation of the non-Western influence being there in the thinking, but not in the sound. This is a more genuine and interesting form of influence because while listening one is not necessarily aware of some non-Western music being imitated. Instead of imitation, the influence of non-Western musical structures on the thinking of a Western composer is likely to produce something genuinely new.[16]

Although he is based in New York, Reich has much in common with the predominantly West Coast composers who seek to replace European music with World music. It should not be forgotten that Americans are in the best position to understand about musical fusions since their country gave birth to the most important of inter-continental syntheses: jazz.

This interest in Eastern cultures pioneered by composers such as Henry Cowell, John Cage and Lou Harrison, has gone from strength to strength. Not only do Javanese, Balinese and Sundanese gamelans abound in America, especially California, with Indonesian teachers in residence, but also some Americans, for example Dennis Murphy, William Colvig, Daniel Schmidt and Paul Dresher have built their own gamelans, from aluminium, scrapped cars, and other materials. Alongside this move towards home-produced instruments is the composition of American pieces for gamelan. Already, quite a large repertoire has been developed which cannot be comprehensively discussed here. Lou Harrison (b. 1917) may be singled out as a key figure. He has the seniority and the technique, developed before he began working with gamelans, to merit particular respect. His work includes music for traditional Western forces, either using procedures from non-Western music or not, as well as what may be classified as 'Gending-gending California'. This is the title of an anthology (privately printed in 1981 by Harrison) of compositions for gamelan by American composers. It is perhaps the ultimate compliment to gamelan music and is far removed from the work of Debussy, Messiaen and Britten. Another important pre-condition which distinguishes such pieces is that the composers are actively involved in playing gamelan and are versed in the theory and practice of Javanese (or Balinese) music. This has led to a reliance on Indonesian models, and the danger is that some of these Western compositions may sound like pastiches of traditional gamelan pieces, but without the deep knowledge of *karawitan* (gamelan music) which is necessary to make them successful. One way that Lou Harrison has found of getting beyond this stage is by incorporating Western instruments (for example, violin, cello, viola, horn, and trumpet) into the gamelan (be it an actual Javanese set or a Harrison–Colvig creation in aluminium and 'just intonation') (regarded as the purest of all tunings because it is based on the natural third and fifth rather than their customary tempered versions). The results can be highly successful: a natural blend or fusion. Of the *Double Concerto for violin, cello and Javanese gamelan* (1981) the veteran gamelan player and teacher in California, Ki Wasitodipuro, remarked to the composer that it sounded just like the old court music.[17]

Interestingly enough, it seems to be Westerners rather than Indonesians who object to such works. First of all, it should be pointed out that the Javanese readily incorporated instruments from the Dutch military bands into their ensembles during the colonial period. Furthermore, it should be remembered how creative and experimental the musicians of Java and Bali can be and how receptive they are to new ideas. Western purists who reject these new pieces should note the following crucial statement from an article by Dennis Murphy:

Dr [David] McAllester [the distinguished ethnomusicologist] has also mentioned to me that when he visited Java, he found the musicians there reasonably interested to learn that there is traditional gamelan in the US but *much* more interested to hear that a few Americans are writing new music for gamelan (and similar orchestras), and that we are making our own instruments to perform this music.[18]

Of course the controversy cannot be laid to rest as easily as this. Anyone steeped in traditional gamelan music is likely to believe that it far surpasses such new pieces, but to reason from this that there is no need to study and play anything else is myopic and contrary to the spirit of a vigorous and dynamic art. What should be conceded is that the traditional masterpieces should be studied not only for their strength and beauty, but also because they afford the best understanding of how the ensemble works. The most successful Western gamelans are therefore, in my opinion, those which combine traditional music (in a spirit of humility and awareness that the performance is unlikely to approach that of an expert Indonesian group) with new pieces which, however tentatively, attempt to break new ground. The two types should develop naturally side by side, and it is regrettable that some groups have chosen one to the exclusion of the other. It is not, after all, as if traditional *karawitan* sprang like pure water from some mysterious source. Creativity and experimentation within cross-cultural frameworks are typical of this and of any other art. Lou Harrison, one of the best possible commentators on this topic, made the following important points in a recent film interview:

> There was a conference in Tokyo in 1962 in which Henry Cowell got up because everybody was being 'pure', and the ethnomusicologists didn't want anybody to touch culture ... And he said 'look, all the hybrids are healthy. They're the ones that grow new things and they make new beauties. So don't put down hybrids.' And so I took that on face value, because of my admiration for the man, until finally it dawned on me, about a year later: don't put down hybrids, because there isn't anything else.[19]

This realization seemed to be the driving force behind an even more significant conference, held at the Indonesian Pavilion at Expo 86 in Vancouver. The symposium and concerts between 18 and 20 August 1986 constituted the First International Gamelan Festival. The international element rested largely on groups from the USA, together with those from Indonesia, Japan, West Germany, and Canada. (No group attended from Britain, although Alec Roth and I participated with other groups.) The musical content tended much more towards new compositions than traditional gamelan music, and some groups took the title 'gamelan' to further limits than are found even in Indonesia, with a repertoire and performance style far different from traditional models, and some instruments radically different from the wide variety which normally goes under the name of gamelan. (In England, the Bow Gamelan would fall into the same category.) The point to make about all this diversity and unashamed experimentation is that it was mainly organized and supported by the Indonesians themselves. The success of this first venture has led to plans for a second festival, in London in the summer of 1990.

In any consideration of the gamelan's world-wide appeal, a third dimension should be added to those of performance and composition. Western involvement with the gamelan has not only centred on the study of traditional Indonesian music and the creation of a new repertoire, but has also exploited the rich benefits to music education. Carl Orff based his Schulwerk instruments on the gamelan, and closer imitations made in America more recently have been widely used in schools. England too, has produced some examples of home-made 'gamelans', among which may be mentioned those of Norman Davis (in a school on Merseyside), Mark Lockett's Metalworks, and Mick Wilson's Cragg Vale Gamelan.

Yet it is no more necessary to have real or imitation instruments in order to reap the benefits of gamelan music than it is for a composer to use actual Indonesian music to demonstrate an affinity with it. In both cases the real values go much deeper. What gamelan music can teach is more than just a novel, exotic musical system; it can develop musicianship at its fundamental and most important level. One of the earliest pioneers of gamelan in the West, who was in fact responsible for initiating performance study under visiting teachers, and who well understood the widest implications of this study, was Mantle Hood:

> We Western musicians can learn much from you, the Javanese *niyaga* [gamelan players]. We can learn something from your methods of musical training, from the rhythmic structure of your *gending*, from the function and preservation of a concept like *patet*, from your voice

control (intonation) in singing, from your gamelan conductor who is heard but not seen, from your feeling for playing in ensemble, from the impersonal quality of your compositions.[20]

A more recent programme of gamelan music in schools was discussed by the teacher Jody Diamond. She made several points which support Mantle Hood's claims, and generally subscribe to the view of gamelan music as an upholder of basic and *universal* aspects of musicianship:

> The gamelan as a learning environment is well suited to some important educational goals: cooperative group interaction, accommodation of individual learning styles and strengths, development of self-confidence, creativity, and musical skills, an integrated study of academic areas, and direct experience of the arts of another culture.[21]

Throughout, Diamond emphasizes co-operation rather than competition, which is the basis of gamelan playing. Because so many of the instruments are easy to play it is possible to operate the gamelan as a perfectly satisfactory mixed ability ensemble. As understanding and technical proficiency develop other instruments can be studied until the student has gained a working knowledge of most, if not all. At any stage, however, the player's basic skills in rhythmic and dynamic co-ordination will be developed, through the primary musical act of listening. Notation can of course be used, but one of the most refreshing things about gamelan music is that it does not depend on visual stimuli. Apart from the obvious value to memory training, matters of balance, tempo and so on depend on the player's ear and corporate sense, rather than on a conductor's baton. This is where gamelan is much closer to jazz, rock and improvised musics than to the Western classical tradition. There is also less interest in the finished artwork by a named composer. Significantly, Diamond stresses the importance of proceeding from a Javanese model to compositions and improvisations by the students themselves. She makes the interesting observation that the *slendro* scale (or their version in just intonation) 'produced few if any unpleasant sounds, which contributed to self-confidence in improvisation'.[22]

It should also be mentioned that the practice of group composition, which assists enormously in the development of creative skills, self-confidence, and corporate sense, is very common in traditional gamelan music, especially in Bali. Usually the composer teaches the outline of the piece (orally) to the rest of the group, who make suggestions and try them out until a satisfactory finished product is reached through a process which, in Java, could be described as group *garap*.

The players are never, therefore, solely the executants of a received repertoire, and the rift between composer and performer, which is unnatural in any society but our own, does not appear. Finally, it should be noted that the children in Diamond's course included many from low-income families who would otherwise not have had the chance to play in an ensemble or to create pieces on which they could work and hear performed.

> And since the cornerstone of my approach to teaching music was to assume that everyone has a basic musical ability that just needs to be brought out, the gamelan program guaranteed some musical training and experience to children who might have been completely over-looked in a more traditional educational setting.[23]

It is hoped that the preceding ideas, as well as the analysis of actual gamelan music, will provide a basis for teachers to develop in their own way. I do not propose to go much beyond this and offer a repertoire of concrete examples for use in the classroom since I would be less qualified to do so than the trained teacher. A few suggestions appear in another publication[24] and many of the principles of gamelan music can be adapted to other instruments. An obvious choice is the Orff percussion, but the diatonic tuning means that one of the crucial dimensions of gamelan music – its unique tuning system – is sacrificed. For this reason, as well as adherence to the Javanese models, it is important not to neglect the contribution that can be made by the voice, as well as by instruments of variable pitch.

Notes

1 Frederick Franck *The Zen of Seeing* (Wildwood House, London, 1973), pp. 9, 44.

2 *The World Encompassed By Sir Francis Drake* (London, Hakluyt Society, 1854), p. 161.

3 Jaap Kunst *Music in Java*, 2 vols. (Martinus Nijhoff, 1973), pp. 5–6.

4 Alexander John Ellis 'On the Musical Scales of Various Nations', *Journal of the Society of Arts* 33, 1885, pp. 485–527.

5 See Edward Lockspeiser *Debussy: his life and mind* Vol. I (Cassell, London, 1962), p. 116, n. 1.

6 Quoted in Lockspeiser, op. cit., p. 115.

7 The only research I know of which proposes a specific relationship between a piece of Debussy and a Javanese gamelan piece is by Richard Mueller, an authority on the music of Colin McPhee. In his article 'Javanese influence on Debussy's *Fantaisie* and beyond', *19th-Century Music* Vol. X, No. 2, Fall 1986, pp. 157–86, he argues that the *Fantaisie* for piano and orchestra (composed between October 1889 and April 1890) uses a Javanese piece entitled *Wani-wani* as the basis of its main cyclic theme. Without going into the merits of the argument, it could be concluded that the exception proved the rule: neither Debussy nor posterity were happy with this work, and one reason could therefore be its adherence to an alien and undigested model. Mueller also draws our attention to an even more obscure undertaking. This was the brief sketch Debussy managed in 1914 for a ballet entitled *No-ja-li*, in which the scenario called for an imitation of a (Malayan) gamelan. The most interesting point about this aborted effort is the date, which is very late in Debussy's career. It is tantalizing to speculate on how his efforts would have compared with Benjamin Britten's similar undertaking (albeit on Balinese models) in his ballet *The Prince of the Pagodas*.

8 For example, first movement: 4 bars before figure 3 (*modéré, sans lenteur*) to around figure 5 (*au mouvement*).

9 See the scores in Kunst, op. cit., pp. 481–9, and the present book, pp. 108–117.

10 Quoted in Lockspeiser, op. cit., p. 115.

11 An appendix in Edward Lockspeiser, op. cit., Vol. II (Cassell, London, 1965), pp. 278–81 discusses the theories of Gaston Bachelard and others on the connections between water and dreams, and their relevance to Debussy and the Symbolist movement.

12 From a letter to Imogen Holst from Ubud, 17 January 1956, quoted in Donald Mitchell and J. Evans, *Benjamin Britten: Pictures from a Life* (London, 1978), p. 297.

13 'An afterword on Britten's "Pagodas": the Balinese sources', *Tempo*, No. 152, March 1985, p. 9, n. 4.

14 Unpublished MA essay, University of York, 1984.

15 'Bertram Turetzky Interviewed' by Leroy Cowie, *Contact* No. 8, Summer 1974, p. 11.

16 Steve Reich *Writings about Music* (Universal Edition, 1974), p. 40.

17 Personal communication, 1985.

18 Dennis Murphy, 'A Shadowplay Tradition in Vermont', *Ear Magazine*, Vol. VIII, No. 4, September/October/November 1983, p. 17.

19 'West Coast Story, 1. Frontiers of new music', BBC TV, 29 November 1986. Significantly, in the background to this interview, was one of Harrison's compositions, for a gamelan which he and William Colvig had built, entitled *Main bersama-sama*, which means 'playing together'.

20 Mantle Hood *The Nuclear Theme as a Determinant of Patet in Javanese Music* (J. B. Wolters, Groningen and Djakarta, 1954), p. viii.
21 Jody Diamond 'Gamelan Programs for Children from the Cross-Cultural to the Creative', *Ear Magazine*, Vol. VIII, No. 4, September/October/November 1983, p. 27.
22 Ibid.
23 Ibid.
24 Graham Vulliamy and Ed Lee, eds. *Pop, Rock and Ethnic Music in School* (Cambridge University Press, 1982), especially Chapter 3.

Chapter 2

The Setting

The best way to begin an account of the actual music is with some observations by the Javanese themselves. The music readily lends itself to poetic imagery, and perhaps the most eloquent tributes emerged in the course of conversations during my first stay in Java (June–August 1971) from which I freely quote:

'The highest form of beauty is stillness.'

'[Gamelan music is like] the raindrops falling from the trees after a shower.'

'When you play the violin [*rebab*] it must be as if there were no violin, only a memory.'

'The best music comes without cause. It is spontaneous, the song of life; therefore it is truly dynamic . . . but music is beyond words.'

How then can one adequately begin to describe these instruments and their sound? Fortunately the dedicated reader is in a position to see and hear them even in this country, and many good recordings are also available (see Suggestions for listening, p.137–9). In Java and Bali, gamelan music seems to hang in the air. It might be heard across the rice-fields at any time of the day or night, and numerous radio broadcasts and a large cassette industry provide an enormous resource. Gamelan music seems to transcend class barriers. It is as much a music of the poorest villager as of the court nobleman, and indeed many of the court musicians and students at urban music academies are from the villages and poorer sections of society. It is the more Westernized affluent urban middle class who are likely to reject gamelan music in favour of Indonesian or Western pop.

18

Gamelan is deeply embedded in the mythology, beliefs and mysticism of the Javanese, and for this reason its sound, which so readily entrances foreigners, reflects values and sensations beyond our comprehension. Yet it does not take long to realize that this is not only one of the most beautiful sounds in the world but also one of the most refined, balanced and civilized of all musical systems. The key to the understanding lies in Javanese culture as a whole, which includes what we might consider everyday behaviour. The Javanese hero is restrained, and much of his power is in direct proportion to that restraint. Sudden outbursts of loud, violent language or aggressive behaviour are considered uncouth and undignified. The quiet, measured and level comportment of the refined hero, described by the important word *alus*, is the ideal to which one aspires, both in life and in art. It says a lot about Javanese values that the *alus* hero is portrayed in puppet plays by small, delicate figures and, in some traditions of live drama, by women. His strength is often a divine gift (he is usually descended from the gods) and his character must be developed and sustained through meditation.

Whatever the history of gamelan may be, the important thing to the Javanese is that it is believed to be of divine origin. The first gong was used as a kind of signalling system among the gods. To this day, animistic beliefs in spirits, especially in the large *gong*, but also in the other instruments, explain the great respect for the gamelan and even its distancing from mortals. (Some old gongs are so revered that they must not even be played, and only approached at certain times in accordance with established ritual.)

An important distinction is often made between the gamelan and the Western symphony orchestra. The gamelan is a set, housed in a special place. The players come to it empty-handed and depart likewise. They will probably remain anonymous, whereas the set of instruments will usually bear a name – a personality which is special to it and serves to identify the whole musical event. The Western orchestra is a collection of individuals (even of individualists!) most of whom bring their own instrument. The musicians are generally specialists in one instrument, whereas a good gamelan player is expected to be proficient in most, if not all, instruments. The cohesion of the ensemble in a symphony orchestra depends on the conductor's ability to blend the instruments into a unit; such a need does not arise with the gamelan since the blend was ensured first at the manufacturing stage, and then by the special rapport between the musicians who know what everyone is playing in the ensemble.

The Western analogy with the gamelan is not, then, the relatively disparate orchestra. Instead we should perhaps consider the question from a new angle: a distinction could be made between instruments which are held or not held. One could then, arguably, regard held instruments as essentially extensions of the human body (and voice) and those which are not held as essentially depersonalized, with sacred connotations. The gamelan is in fact hardly touched at all. It is the mallets which make the contact, and only on some instruments are the hands used, usually in the secondary function of damping. It is this all-important intervention of mallets between human and instrument which has given the gamelan its name, since the word is usually translated as the action (–an) of a hammer (gamel). This priority is reinforced by taboos associated with the gamelan: removal of polluting outdoor footwear and the avoidance of all foot contact with the instruments, and even of stepping over them. In all cases the main consideration seems to be the respectful detachment of player from instrument and his subservience, as to an object with sacred or mystical associations or to the spirits of his ancestors. This notion of detachment, iklas, is central to Javanese attitudes and helps explain much about the behaviour, emotional restraint, and consequent aesthetic priorities of the people. Although we should beware of ascribing a sacred aspect, or at least the same one, to all gamelans, it does seem that the nearest among the admittedly distant analogies in our own culture might be found in churches, rather than in concert halls. The bells above and the organ below are both housed in the building; the ropes intervene between ringers and bells, and the organ keys serve to unlock the sound. Of course, bells do not provide the varied musical repertoire of a gamelan, and the organ is essentially a one-man band which depends on an array of gadgetry quite alien to the beautiful simplicity of the gamelan. Yet the sacred associations, fixed position, and the identification of the instruments, sometimes to the exclusion of the player(s), and the further detachment of the player(s), who neither hold nor own the instruments, do provide interesting parallels with the gamelan and perhaps help the Westerner to understand its peculiar significance.

To extend this analogy a little further before leaving it, such instruments may be used to give musical enjoyment, but this is not their only function, and in certain cases it may even be a subsidiary consideration.

For example, church bells are a signal, and the organ is used mostly as an accompaniment to sacred texts. The gamelan's mythical origins are as a kind of celestial signalling system, its earliest repertoire probably developed as an accompaniment to classical poetry, and today one of its main functions – arguably the main one – remains as an accompaniment (*iringan*) to various Javanese mythical theatrical genres.

To consider this subject in any detail is well beyond the scope of this book. Gamelan pieces (*gendhing*) may be classified according to their usage, thus *gendhing klenengan* are the equivalent of concert music, *gendhing beksan* are to accompany dance (*iringan tari*), *gendhing wayangan* are used in the *wayang* puppet plays, and *gendhing pakurmatan* (from a word meaning honour or reverence) are for ceremonial functions and tend to use restricted scales and instrumentations reminiscent of the old ceremonial gamelans.[1] Sometimes *gendhings* are also classified according to mood: *gendhing gecul* (funny or mischievous) or *gendhing gobyog* referring to cheerful, even humorous pieces, and *gendhing tlutur* or *welasan* to sad or pitiful ones. Perhaps the main point to underline is the close interconnection of the arts in Java, which is quite common throughout Asia but much less so in Europe. The equivalent of a music academy (in Solo, Central Java) in fact comprises three sections: for music, dance, and puppetry. In the West the close connection between music and dance has waned, yet still the two arts flourish on equal, if separate, terms; but what of puppetry?

If this art has become associated in the West with children's entertainment, then in Java at least it is certainly true that the child is father of the man. It is here that we find the essence and summation of Javanese culture – a *Gesamtkunstwerk* that makes Wagner's seem experimental and incomplete; and the Javanese example has the added important advantage of a long and deep relevance to all levels of society. The Javanese shadow play, called *wayang kulit*, (abbreviated to *wayang*), is more than a total art work: it is a ritual, enshrining myth and the religion of Java before Islam, whose purpose is not only to entertain but also to instruct, and to mark the important stages of the life-cycle and events of communal significance. The *dhalang* (puppeteer) becomes an intermediary between humans and gods. In society he has a special position and respect, while in the *wayang* performance itself he is omnipotent.[2] Everything is controlled by him: he narrates the entire story, providing all the dialogue, singing the important *suluk* (special chants of *wayang*), manipulating the puppets, and directing the gamelan behind him through an elaborate system of cues, some of which are clear and others deliberately veiled. These cues are given in a variety of ways. Some are spoken or sung, while others are communicated through the *dhalang*'s own percussion ensemble, comprising a mallet with which he strikes the side of the puppet box, another which he grips between his toes, and a set of metal plates (*kepyak*) which he strikes with his foot!

The poetry of allusion and allegory, mixed with the extremes of spiritual refinement and downright bawdiness, are typical of the range of language in *wayang*. Moreover, the meditations and noble deeds of heroes and gods, or the antics and robust humour of the clowns, are not restricted to this and related theatrical forms, but permeate behaviour models in Javanese society. *Wayang* has always been an effective vehicle of propaganda, from the mythical association of its heroes from the Hindu *Mahabharata* and *Ramayana* epics with the kings of Java, to its use of political slogans and symbols in modern Indonesia. Few art forms in the world combine so much to communicate on so many levels to such a wide spectrum of society. Yet the external trappings are relatively simple: a screen, attached to a rectangular wooden frame, a suspended lamp (nowadays electric, but traditionally a more atmospheric flickering oil lamp), two banana logs into which the puppets are fixed by means of a sharp horn spike at their base, and of course the puppets themselves. Here the crafts of leather carving and painting are applied to produce exquisite shapes from thin, flat pieces of hide. As was noted earlier, the strongest and most heroic characters are among the smallest and most delicately carved puppets. In their manipulation the *dhalang* must understand the art of Javanese dance. Many of the postures and movements of dance are derived from *wayang*, and a prominent theatrical genre is in effect *wayang* using live actors and actresses, appropriately known in Javanese as *wayang wong*, or in its Indonesian translation as *wayang orang* (human *wayang*). Nowadays, however, it is performed in theatres for a paying public, and its length is less than half that of the traditional *wayang kulit* performance, which begins at around 9 p.m. and goes on without a break until just before dawn. The gamelan music for *wayang kulit* is not continuous, neither is, necessarily, the presence and attention of the audience/spectators; but the *dhalang* must remain and perform in his special cross-legged seated position for the entire eight or nine hours. It is not to relieve the pressure on the *dhalang* but rather on the audience, that shorter *wayang*s, of only a couple of hours, have become more widespread.

The gamelan accompaniment to *wayang* may be intermittent, but it is far from incidental. The whole *lakon* (play) is a large cyclic structure in three main parts, and the music is totally integrated into this scheme. Traditionally the *slendro* tuning is used, and the three main sections correspond to the three *pathets* (sub-tonalities, or note-hierarchies) of the *slendro* tuning: *nem*, *sanga*, and *manyura*. (These are explained in Chapter 4.) The resultant gradual ascent in tessitura relates to the *lakon* as an allegory of the life-cycle and the gradual attainment of experience and enlightenment.

The use of Hindu mythology, albeit thoroughly assimilated into Javanese culture through the *wayang* and other art-forms, is one of the main examples of Indian influence (also found extensively in other parts of south-east Asia). If the modern Republic of Indonesia, of which Java is the centre, has taken 'Unity in Diversity' as its motto and achieved amazing results, it is the very diversity and richness of culture in the archipelago which attracts and even bewilders us.

Java seems to have been one of the first places to be inhabited by humans. Between about 5000 and 2000 BC migrants from the main-land of western China and the Malay peninsula dominated the indigen-ous population. The early centuries of our Christian era saw the arrival of traders from India and the absorption of Hindu and Buddhist culture. Obvious vestiges remain today in the spectacular Hindu temple com-plex at Prambanan and the Buddhist stupa of Borobudur, both por-traying several musical instruments of Indian origin which have not endured in the modern gamelan. In fact, *karawitan* (gamelan music) has remarkably few affinities with Indian music, either in its priorities and organization or its terminology. Occasionally the title of a piece shows the impact of Sanskrit on the Javanese language, '*Puspawarna*' (kinds of flowers) being a good example, but it is in religion, mythology and, of course, language that the Indian influence is felt. The so-called Hindu–Javanese period was a golden age, establishing what is now both Jav-anese and Balinese culture. The bifurcation was largely the result of the advent of Islam. Again, it was mainly through the agency of Indian traders that this religion came to Java. By the end of the fifteenth century, the great Hindu–Javanese Majapahit Empire had collapsed and

Islam became established as the main religion in Java. Even today, the Republic of Indonesia has the largest Muslim population in the world. Rather than submit, the Javanese nobles of the Majapahit Empire fled across the narrow strait to Bali, which then continued as a repository of Hindu–Javanese culture, and is today the only predominantly Hindu land outside the Indian subcontinent. It also managed to avoid Dutch rule, which had spread throughout Java and neighbouring islands since the early seventeenth century, until 1906. The colonialists did not stay in their East Indies much longer, being driven out first by the Japanese in 1942 and finally by the Indonesians themselves between 1945 and 1949. When the Dutch began their domination, Central Java was ruled by the second Mataram kingdom, whose greatest leader, Sultan Agung, died in 1645. Thereupon the kingdom became increasingly dependent on Dutch support until the Europeans finally used their influence to divide it in 1755. A *kraton* (court) was established in the two capitals of Surakarta (still more commonly known by its original name of Solo) and Yogyakarta (abbreviated to Jogja), which lie about forty miles apart. Later, second courts were established in each city, first the Mangkunegaran in Solo and then, during the brief period near the end of the Napoleonic wars when Britain took control from the Dutch, the Pakualaman in Jogja. Despite a shared Central Javanese culture, and even family relationships between the royal houses, the Solonese and Jogjanese styles and repertoires of gamelan music, *wayang* and so on have remained distinct, and the spirit of rivalry between them persists even today when the power of the courts has all but vanished. Cultural life still finds an important base in the *kraton*s, which maintain gamelans and dancers. But dances which used to be restricted to the court are now taught in dance schools and publicly performed, while many of the court musicians also play in the gamelan at the local station of Radio Republik Indonesia (RRI), or even travel abroad to teach the growing number of Westerners studying gamelan. Major institutions were set up in Jogja, Solo, Den Pasar (Bali) and other cultural centres to widen the study of music, dance, puppetry, and other related art-forms, within the framework of the new Indonesian state. Not only education but also creativity needed to serve this broader national aim, as composers and choreographers sought new ways of addressing mass audiences. Contrary to the Western idea of placid, unchanging oriental traditions (because, after all, much does endure serenely), things *do* change, and perhaps nowhere more dramatically than in Bali.

Although this book is not concerned with Balinese music, which would merit at least as much attention, it is important to mention one or two things, if only to ensure that the listener will be able to distinguish Balinese gamelan from Javanese. (On more than one occasion the BBC, assuming that gamelan is gamelan regardless of where it comes from, has used recordings of Balinese music to illustrate points about Javanese music, and vice versa.) The typical modern gamelans of each island are very different, both in sound and appearance. The larger Central Javanese gamelan, with both *slendro* and *pelog* tunings, plays generally slow, dignified and gentle music. Much of Balinese music shares these traits, but the early years of this century saw a revolution in Bali no less dramatic than the contemporaneous rise of jazz in the West. Choreographers and musicians developed a new dance and accompanying musical style called *kebyar*, which means something like 'bursting forth', and is aptly named. At first in the north and later all over the small island, this new style – characterized by great exuberance, dramatic starts and stops, dynamic contrasts, rhythmic complexity and overt group virtuosity – became the kind of music for which Bali is now best known. This new gamelan (actually a somewhat rare word to the Balinese, who tend to prefer to call the ensemble 'gong') developed from the older and larger ensemble called *(gamelan) gong gedhe*. The tuning is *pelog*, but five notes are available rather than the seven of Java. (The tuning systems are explained in Chapter 4.) The Balinese scale approximates to the notes 1 2 3 5 6 of the Javanese *pelog* tuning. *Slendro* is found in Bali, and, as in Java, is associated with *wayang kulit*. The accompaniment is provided on a quartet of *gender*s, called *gender wayang*, which are similar to their Javanese counterparts but with an important feature which typifies the difference between Javanese and Balinese music. Whereas the Javanese *gender* is played with padded mallets and gives a soft, mellow sound, the Balinese *gender wayang* are struck with 'naked' wooden mallets, which give a much louder and brighter sound. It is worth remembering that Balinese music is essentially an outdoor music, while the Javanese gamelan, at least in the courts, is played in a reverberant pavilion. Another major *slendro* ensemble in Bali is the four-note *gamelan angklung*, which again is played outdoors and even on the move, for temple processions and the like. Another processional ensemble, the *gamelan bebonangan*, is used to accompany cremations. This shows the Balinese ingenuity for complex interlocking patterns: the ensemble is made up of large gongs, cymbals, and small gongs (*bonang*), each player carrying one and contributing an ostinato to the resulting complex pattern. A vocal equivalent to this is the famous *kecak*, in which men predominantly chant the syllable 'cak' in a very exciting interlocking chorus. The richness and intensity of artistic life in Bali, and the extraordinary diversity of the gamelans and other ensembles, can only be marvelled at here, rather than discussed in any detail.

Before returning to Central Java and the Solonese style of *karawitan* which is the focus of this book, mention should be made of the fact that gamelan music is not simply divided between Java and Bali. We have already noted that, even on the small island of Bali, there are many differing ensembles which can go under the name of gamelan. The name is also found outside Indonesia altogether, for example in Malaysia; and in Java itself we can distinguish at least two major traditions, which can in turn be subdivided. The island is divided into three main provinces: Jawa Barat (West Java), Jawa Tengah (Central Java), and Jawa Timur (East Java). West Java contains the capital of Indonesia, Jakarta, and, to the south-east, the region of Sunda, centred on Bandung. This not only has its own language but also its distinctive and very beautiful gamelan style. One of the main characteristics is a highly ornamented vocal style, which is also adapted to wind and stringed instruments, using notes outside the fixed pitches of the gamelan to great expressive effect. Central Java, which for cultural purposes includes the Daerah Istimewa Yogyakarta (the Special Area of Yogyakarta), contains the major Javanese gamelan traditions of Solo and Jogja, and also of the regional capital, Semarang. East Java has close cultural links with Central Java, as well as several regional styles of its own, including those of Surabaya (Indonesia's second city), and of Banyuwangi, the nearest town to Bali. Many of the finest gamelan players in Solo actually come from East Java. In confining ourselves to Central Java, particularly Solo, we are not, therefore, talking about 'the gamelan', but, at the most, a *primus inter pares*.

Notes

1 This is a large topic outside the scope of this book, since the old ceremonial gamelans, housed in the palaces, are not in everyday use (each one tends to be restricted to a specific function or event), nor do they play the kind of music associated with the modern gamelan. Many of their instruments are similar to the modern versions, but as a very general rule those of the older ensembles are fewer in number but larger in size.

2 The use of the masculine pronoun is deliberate. *Dhalang*s are traditionally male, but it is interesting to note that there are some women exponents of this art. We should also note here that, while there have always been female musicians in Java, gamelan players are traditionally male. In recent times, however, large numbers of women have taken up playing, not only in the West, but also in Java, where mixed groups, and also '*Ibu-ibu*' (all-women) groups are common. Singers and dancers are of both sexes, according to the context.

Chapter 3

The Instruments

Despite the changes over the centuries, and the diversity which still exists today, the modern complete Javanese gamelan is standardized enough for one to talk about a typical ensemble. The majority of instruments are made of metal (usually bronze but very often iron) which is struck with different kinds of mallets (*tabuh*). These instruments may be divided into two structural groups: *wilah* (bars, plates) and *pencon* (knobbed instruments, that is mainly gongs). To give them their complete name, both words may be preceded by the word *ricik* or *ricikan* (meaning tools and gamelan instruments) although Tentrem Sarwanto, the maker of Gamelan Sekar Pethak, the set housed in York, preferred the word *bunderan* (sphere) to *ricikan* in conjunction with *pencon*, no doubt to distinguish the round shape of *pencon* instruments (gongs) from the rectangular shape of *wilah*.

The typical gamelan has approximately 156 individual bronze *wilah* and 75 *pencon*. This assumes that the set is in effect a double gamelan, incorporating instruments in both of the Javanese tuning systems, *slendro* and *pelog* (which are discussed further in Chapter 4). The *wilah* instruments include the *saron* and *gender* families (and also the *gambang*, with wooden bars). Two kinds of (metal) *wilah* are involved. (A third type, *wilah pencon*, characterized by a central knob, thus combining features of *wilah* and *pencon*, is still found, through not in the typical modern gamelan under discussion.) The *saron* type, *wilah polos* or *lugas* (simple, unadorned, referring to the smooth surface) is a thick, slightly curved bar, and all such *wilah* constituting one instrument are mounted over a single trough resonator. The mallets used are hard (wood or horn) and the playing may be loud or soft. The *gender* type, *wilah blimbingan* (named after the star-fruit *averrhoa bilimbi*, presumably because of the more jagged surface, compared to the *wilah polos* type) is a thin, ribbed plate, and each one is suspended over a tube resonator, or *bumbung*, which is tuned to the pitch of that particular *wilah*. The mallets have a head in the shape of a disc which is covered by a detachable ring of padding, and the strokes are usually gentle.

All *pencon* are (circular) gongs with a central protruding boss called *pencu* (the two words, *pencon* and *pencu*, are in fact virtually synonymous) which is struck during playing. As with the *wilah* instruments the *pencon* instruments may also be broadly divided into two types. The two distinguishing words, *gandhul* and *pangkon*, literally refer to the way in which the gongs are supported, rather than to their shape, but the two factors are broadly complementary, with some exceptions. *Gandhul* literally means 'hanging', and *pangkon* means 'cradled'. Hanging gongs are suspended from a wooden bar so that the *pencu* is on the side, while cradled gongs are supported from the base (the open rim) by cords, so that the *pencu* points upwards. (The rim is a node and therefore this method of support does not damp the sound.) The large *pencon gandhul* are struck with mallets that have more or less spherical heads of heavy padding, while all *pencon pangkon* are struck with sticks that are lightly padded with coiled string.

The large *pencon gandhul* instruments are the *gong ageng*, *gong suwukan* and *kempul*. Their shape is characterized by a flat surface around the *pencu*, becoming slightly concave near the edge. Smaller versions – the *kethuk* and the lower-pitched gongs on the *bonang barung* and *bonang panerus* – are literally *pangkon* (cradled, rather than hung) although they have the same shape as the large *pencon gandhul*. The other *pencon pangkon* gongs are the higher-pitched gongs on the other *bonang*s, the *kempyang*s (which are always part of a set with the *kethuk*s) and all the *kenong*s. Their shape is distinguished by a surface which slopes up to the *pencu*. Gongs with this shape are always supported from below, and, as has already been explained, several gongs of the flatter shape associated with the large *pencon gandhul* are also supported in this way.

These broad distinctions are shown in Figure 1, and the following description of the individual instruments which comprise the metal idiophone section of the gamelan will be according to these four divisions.

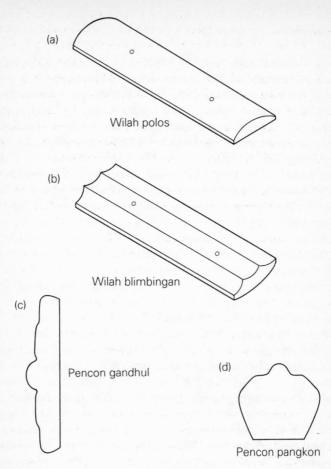

(a) Wilah polos

(b) Wilah blimbingan

(c) Pencon gandhul

(d) Pencon pangkon

Figure 1

The word used for the wooden cases and racks of the gamelan is *rancak*, and the wood most commonly used is teak (*jati*). The *rancak* are often carved with floral motifs and intertwined serpents, and are usually painted: the carvings in gold and the rest in one other colour, usually red, blue, green or black. Neither carving nor painting is essential and many gamelans exist with simple carving or none at all, while a small minority are unpainted.

Wilah polos

The *saron* family, together with the *slenthem*, make up the section which performs the fixed melody (*balungan*) of the composition (discussed in Chapter 4). Taking the register of the *saron barung* as a reference, the *saron panerus* (more usually known by its nickname *peking*) is pitched an octave higher, and the *saron demung* (known simply as *demung*) an octave lower. (The *slenthem* is an octave below the *demung*.) Thus the *wilah* of the *peking* are smaller than those of the *saron barung*, and those of the *demung* are larger. The measurements of the smallest *peking wilah* are approximately 18 cm long by 4 cm wide[1], while those of the largest *demung wilah* are approximately 35.5 cm long by 9 cm wide. The *peking wilah* are, however, relatively thick. As the pitch rises the arch of the *wilah* also rises, so that the thickness (at the centre) of the smallest *peking wilah* is approximately 2.5 cm while that of the largest *demung wilah* is approximately 1 cm. A hole is drilled at a nodal point near each end of the *wilah*. Pins, inserted into the wooden case, pass through these holes, securing the *wilah* over the resonator, which is a trough cut into the *rancak*. The *wilah*, however, have to be cushioned from the wood, otherwise a large area would be damped. The pins pass through small squares of plaited ratan (or any other effective material, such as cloth padding, cork or rubber) and the *wilah* rest on them.

The *saron* family (plus the *slenthem*) usually have seven *wilah*, whether *slendro* or *pelog* (these tuning systems are discussed in Chapter 4). Thus each of the *pelog* notes is present while two of the *slendro* notes are duplicated at the octave. (*Pelog* is a heptatonic system, while *slendro* is pentatonic). The *slendro* sequence is 6 1 2 3 5 6 i (the dots indicating notes in the octave above or below). In some gamelans one of the *slendro saron*s has nine *wilah*, with ż and ʒ being added to the sequence. This is to allow the performance of *nyacah* (divisions, kinds of variation patterns) which are frequently played in the *wayang* puppet plays, especially in the types of piece called *srepegan* and *sampak*. The instrument is therefore known as *saron wayang*, and sometimes also as *saron wilah sanga* (*sanga* meaning nine).

The mallets of the *saron barung* and *demung* are similar, (though that of the *demung* is considerably larger), and consist of a stick and detachable, barrel-shaped head which is secured to the stick by a hole drilled about halfway through. Occasionally the end of the stick must be wetted or paper wrapped around it to ensure a tight fit in the hole. In extreme cases, a nail is inserted through the head into the stick. These are in fact the only mallets in the Javanese gamelan made solely of wood and where wood is in direct contact with the metal during playing. The thickness of the *wilah* requires a hard mallet and relatively strong blows. In the case of the *peking* the greater thickness of the *wilah* requires an even harder mallet, and for this instrument alone a buffalo horn is used for the head. This ensures a bright, slightly piercing sound, even in soft playing, and so the *peking* should never be struck forcefully.

The *saron* and *demung* possess the greatest dynamic range in the gamelan, from soft, almost inaudible playing, to the exhilarating sound that dominates the ensemble in the *soran* (loud) style. The mallet is gripped in the right hand and, in the case of the *saron* and *demung*, the head strikes the *wilah* at an angle with a slightly glancing blow to ensure maximum resonance. The other hand is used to damp the *wilah* as the next one is being struck. This is usually done by pinching the end of the *wilah* between the thumb and forefinger, and this combination of striking and damping, often necessitating the crossing of the hands, is the only technical difficulty of these instruments. In certain vigorous pieces a special effect called *ngencot* is called for. This is a dry sound obtained by striking (twice) a *wilah* which is simultaneously damped, and is a speciality of the Jogjanese tradition. These techniques of holding the mallet and damping the *wilah* apply to the *slenthem* which is musically in the same group as the *saron* family, but structurally in the *gender* family, and therefore discussed in the following section.

Wilah blimbingan

As has been noted, the shape of the *wilah blimbingan* and the method of mounting them are different from the *wilah polos* family. Instead of resting the *wilah* over a common trough resonator, each *wilah* of the *slenthem* and *gender* is suspended over an individual tuned tube resonator. A section of a single length of cord is passed through the hole at each end of the *wilah* and secured underneath by a small piece of wood rather like a thick matchstick. (Formerly these pieces, called *bremara*, were made of horn, and were of a different shape which was tapered to the middle.) The cord between each *wilah* is supported by a metal hook (*sanggan*) inserted into the wooden frame and protruding about 5 cm above it. The cord itself is secured at each end of the frame. The system is not unlike that of the Western orchestral vibraphone or xylophone, except that the Javanese method of suspension permits much more movement of the *wilah*, sometimes resulting in its accidental striking against its adjacent *sanggan*.

The resonators (*bumbung*) look virtually identical from a distance but since each one is tuned there are important differences in terms of the dimension of the aperture at the top and the distance at which the tube is internally stopped. More will be said on this subject in the section on tuning later in this chapter. The *bumbung* used to be made of bamboo, but fortunately for those gamelans in the West, where the changes of climate would cause a rapid deterioration of such a fragile material, the practice nowadays is to use metal (zinc) which is then painted (usually in a yellow colour to give it the appearance of extraordinarily smooth and regular bamboo).

The *slenthem*, used to play the fixed melody (*balungan*) along with the *saron* family, has the same number of *wilah* and range as the other *balungan* instruments, albeit in a lower octave. Its *wilah*s and *bumbung*s are larger than those of the *gender barung*, which, in their turn, are larger than those of the *gender panerus*. The largest *wilah* of the *slenthem* measures approximately 36 cm long by 9.5 cm wide, while the smallest *wilah* of the *gender panerus* measures approximately 15 cm long by 4 cm wide. The *slenthem* is played with a similar technique to the other *balungan* instruments (the *saron* group), using a single mallet of which the head is a wooden disc encircled by a thick ring of felt. The *gender barung* and *gender panerus*, however, belong to the group of instruments which embellish the *balungan*, although they are structurally similar to the *slenthem*. The main difference, apart from musical function, is in the number of *wilah* and mallets. A *gamelan seprangkat* (double gamelan, comprising instruments in both the *slendro* and *pelog* tunings) will also have three – rather than two – *gender barung* and three *gender panerus*: one in *slendro* and two in *pelog*. The *pelog* instruments differ only by one note. One instrument has the notes 7 2 3 5 6 and the other the notes 1 2 3 5 6. (This difference is to do with the sub-scales and tonalities (*pathet*) of each tuning system, which are discussed in Chapter 4.) In both cases the note 4 in *pelog* is omitted. It can be mentioned here that the same applies to the *gambang*, but on that instrument the *wilah* are mounted in such a way that a substitution (just between the notes 1 and 7) can be made easily and quickly on the same *rancak*. Such a substitution on the *genders*, although not unheard of, is extremely difficult, and for this reason it is necessary to use separate *rancak, wilah* and *bumbung*.

Each *gender* has fourteen *wilah* and a range from low 6 to high 3, in both *slendro* and *pelog*. (Some *gender*, however, have only 12 or 13 *wilah*.) The *gender panerus* is pitched an octave above the *gender barung*, and the three instruments are consequently smaller than their *gender barung* counterparts. Musically the *gender barung* is by far the more important, but the playing technique is essentially the same on both instruments. They are among the most difficult in the gamelan because two mallets, similar to the *slenthem* mallet but smaller and with a much shorter handle, must be used. Because of this, damping the *wilah* becomes much more difficult and it is necessary to hold the mallets in a special manner. The little finger, thumb and edge of the hand are thus variously available for damping, so the player is effectively doing four things at once: striking two *wilah* and damping two others. Very often, however, the *gender panerus* avoids playing two simultaneous lines, which is why it is easier to play than the *gender barung*, even though its part generally moves at twice the speed. This will be examined further in Chapter 5.

Pencon gandhul: gong ageng, gong suwukan, kempul

The many gongs of different sizes in the *gamelan* have already been divided into two main types: the hanging *pencon gandhul* and the cradled *pencon pangkon*. All gongs, with the exception of the *bonang barung* and the *bonang panerus*, perform what is often termed a 'colotomic' (phrasing or punctuating) function in the music, which will be discussed in the next two chapters. It is an interesting fact that these colotomic gongs have onomatopoeic names, including 'gong' itself. In most cases it is the second syllable (on which the stress occurs) which imitates the sound: kem*pul*, ke*nong*, ke*thuk*, kem*pyang*. The largest gongs which hang in one or two large stands (essentially two side posts

supporting a crossbar) at the back of the gamelan are the *gong ageng,*
gong suwukan and *kempul.* Because they are the only gongs that are
hung rather than supported from below, it is necessary for the manufacturer to drill two holes in the rim, through which is attached a strong
piece of cord with a loop at either end. One loop is pushed through the
other and secured on the crossbar of the wooden stand by a small
wooden toggle, called *cakilan.* The number of gongs suspended in this
way varies from gamelan to gamelan. Usually there will be at least one
gong ageng which is the largest (*ageng* means 'large'), lowest-pitched,
most respected and certainly most expensive item in the gamelan. *Gong
ageng* can vary quite considerably in size, hence in pitch which is often
beautifully at variance with all the other pitches of the gamelan. The
gong ageng of Gamelan Sekar Pethak is approximately 85 cm in
diameter and tuned to around note 6, which is slightly smaller and
higher than the best old gongs. The next largest gong is the *gong
suwukan,* which in certain kinds of music is used as a substitute for the
gong ageng. A typical gamelan will have one *suwukan,* tuned to *slendro*
2 and quite often there will be a second *suwukan,* tuned to *slendro* 1,
and of a similar size of approximately 63 cm in diameter.

The other hanging gongs are collectively called *kempul.* The number
of *kempul* is not standardized, since the notes of both scales do not all
have to be represented. The typical modern gamelan will have a *kempul*
tuned to the note 6 (serving both *pelog* and *slendro*) and others tuned to
pelog 5, *slendro* 5, *pelog* 1, *slendro* 1 and *pelog* 7 (both notes 1, and 7 in
pelog lying above the 6 of the *kempul* tuned to that note). In many
gamelans a *kempul* tuned to note 3 (*slendro* and/or *pelog*) is found, but,
if not, *kempul* 6 may be used to accompany notes 3 or 2 (either *slendro*
or *pelog*) in the melody. (The *suwukan,* tuned to 2, cannot be used as a
kempul, but it is not uncommon to find a *kempul* tuned to the 2 an
octave above this note.) The smallest gong in the Gamelan Sekar Pethak
stand, the *kempul* tuned to *pelog* 1, measures approximately 45 cm in
diameter. All these gongs are struck with mallets consisting of a ball of
heavy padding on a short wooden handle. The padding is usually in
three sizes: the largest for the *gong ageng,* the middle size for the *gong
suwukan,* and the smallest for the *kempul.* The fleshy side of the
clenched fist serves as a good alternative in the case of the larger gongs.

Pencon pangkon: kenong

All other gongs in the gamelan are supported from below, with the central boss (*pencu*) pointing upwards, and are struck with mallets consisting of a stick with padding made of coiled string. The largest such gongs are the *kenong* which are all *pencon pangkon*. The *rancak* are like two boxes open at the top and bottom and sharing a common side. Across the top, from each corner, are attached two pieces of stout cord which cross diagonally and serve as the support for the *kenong*s. Since the usual number of *kenong*s nowadays is ten there are five such *rancak* (although in some gamelans there are *rancak*s for three *kenong*s, so the arrangement for the same number of ten *kenong*s would be two such *rancak*s, plus two sets of the dual *rancak* described above). It should be noted that although all gongs in the gamelan require some kind of support, none requires a resonator. If a *pencon pangkon* has a weaker sound than its neighbours, however, it is rested on a banana leaf or thin sheet of paper as a simple yet effective remedy.

It is generally accepted that the size of gamelan instruments has diminished but their number has increased over the centuries. Nowadays it is common to find a *kenong* for each note of *pelog* and *slendro*. As with the *kempul*s, the notes 1 (*slendro* and *pelog*) are pitched above the note 6, and *slendro* 5 may be borrowed to do service as *pelog* 4 if required. This assumes that the two tuning systems coincide on note 6, which is most often the case (including Gamelan Sekar Pethak). The fact that there are usually more *kenong*s than *kempul*s seems to reflect their relative importance: all pieces require *kenong*s but not all require *kempul*s.

The height, from the rim to the top of the boss, is approximately 32 cm, and the (maximum) diameter approximately 34 cm in the case of the smallest *kenong* (*pelog* 1). The largest *kenong* (*slendro* 2) has a similar height, though the diameter is approximately 37 cm.

Kethuk-kempyang, bonang barung, bonang panerus

The *kethuk* and *kempyang* are usually placed next to the *kenong* (sometimes played by the same musician) and rest on similar (though smaller) *rancak*. There is a set of one *kethuk* and one *kempyang* for each tuning system. The *kempyang* is never played without the *kethuk*, whereas in certain kinds of composition the *kethuk* alone is used. The *kethuk*, similar in shape to the *pencon gandhul*, but with a flat surface from *pencu* to edge, is the lower-pitched of the pair, tuned to note 6 for music in *pelog* and to *slendro* 2 for music in *slendro*. The *kempyang*, shaped like a small *kenong*, is tuned to note 6 (an octave above the *pelog kethuk*) for music in *pelog*, and to *slendro* i (a seventh above the *slendro kethuk*) for music in *slendro*.

The other instruments which mix *pencon gandhul* and *pencon pangkon* shapes are the *bonang barung* and *bonang panerus*, which are gong-chimes comprising two rows of gongs smaller than the *kethuk* and *kempyang*. On these instruments the lowest notes are *pencon gandhul*-shaped, and the shape of the gongs gradually changes to that of the typical *pencon pangkon* (for example, the *kenong*) as the pitches rise. The smallest gong on the *bonang panerus*, (hence in the gamelan), a *pencon pangkon* tuned to *slendro* i, is approximately 17.5 cm in diameter. (For comparison, the larger *kempyang* measures approximately 24 cm in diameter and the larger *kethuk*, both gongs in *pelog*, is approximately 26.5 cm.) The *bonang rancak*s resemble small bedframes with a number of open squares through which pass two parallel lengths of cord. The gongs rest in these individual squares and are supported by the cords. The typical *pelog bonang* (*barung* and *panerus*) has fourteen gongs (two rows of seven) while the *slendro* pair have twelve gongs (two rows of six). In each case the gongs are placed so that octaves lie diagonally around the pivotal octave between the two notes 3, which are directly opposite, and the player sits in line with these notes and holds a mallet in each hand. This arrangement is shown below (Figures 2 and 3). (The *bonang barung* and *bonang panerus* are laid out in the same way, with the gongs of the *bonang panerus* correspondingly an octave above those of the *bonang barung*, and are thus smaller.)

4	6	5	3	2	7	1
1	7	2	3	5	6	4

player

6	5	3	2	1	2
1	2	3	5	6	1

player

Figure 2 bonang pelog   *Figure 3 bonang slendro*

(The position of the notes 1 and 7 may be exchanged to facilitate easier access to whichever is the more important note in the piece. The above layout is for pieces using 7 more than 1, hence the 7 is within easier reach of the player.)

The parts played on these instruments are far more elaborate than the kinds of punctuation performed by the other gongs, and involve elaborations of the skeletal melody, which will be discussed in Chapter 5.

Other instruments

The remaining instruments do not use bronze as the main material in their construction and form a miscellany whose musical function is of utmost importance. Before discussing them, two more bronze instruments with subsidiary roles and which are neither *wilah* nor *pencon*, may be mentioned. The *kecer* is a set of two small bronze cymbals, measuring approximately 9.5 cm in diameter, set in a small solid *rancak*, and two more cymbals, tied together with string and held in each hand, which are used to strike the two in the *rancak* with a staccato, muted action. This instrument can be used in certain types of lighter, lively music but its presence is not essential. The *kemanak*, on the other hand, must be used to accompany certain kinds of vocal piece, often in conjunction with dance, but is otherwise not much used in gamelan music. The set comprises two *kemanak*s, tuned to 6 and the *slendro* 1 above it, and two players are normally required, each striking one *kemanak* with a *bonang panerus* mallet. The *kemanak* is made from a single plate of bronze, curled to give the shape of a banana with a short handle. The two edges of the plate almost meet, leaving a slit near which the mallet strikes. The *kemanak* is held in the hand, and the thumb can be used to cover one end of the slit, producing a sudden stopping and slight lowering of the pitch. The two instruments, played alternately, produce no more than a simple ostinato figure to accompany the vocal melody. Another instrument may be briefly mentioned, if only because of its ingenuity. This is the *gong kemodhong* which may, not unfairly, be described as a poor man's *gong ageng*, since it is simple to make and uses only a fraction of the metal. It is used as a substitute for the *gong ageng*, usually in the reduced, softer ensemble called *gadhon*, and never in conjunction with it. Two plates with a central boss (examples of the obsolescent *wilah pencon* type mentioned earlier) are suspended over a box resonator. The secret lies in the acoustic phenomenon of beats (which is much exploited in the Balinese gamelan). The two plates are slightly different in tuning, so that when they are struck one after the other a low throbbing sound, similar to that of the *gong ageng*, is produced.

The 'non-bronze' miscellany of instruments includes the two regarded by the Javanese as the nearest equivalents to directors of the gamelan. ('Conductor', with its connotation of visual stimulus, can never be used in connection with gamelan.) They are the two-stringed fiddle, *rebab*, and the drum set, *kendhang*. Because of its Arabic name (instruments called *rabab*, or similar names, are found throughout the Muslim world) the *rebab* is generally thought to be more clearly of foreign origin and recent addition to the gamelan than the other instruments. It is a spike fiddle with an almost heart-shaped body made of wood and covered with a thin and delicate skin taken from the intestine or bladder of a buffalo. The two copper strings are tuned by two exaggeratedly long and ornate pegs (which would break if gripped anywhere other than close to the neck of the instrument). The strings pass over a wide-based wooden bridge, and are secured around the bottom of the stick. As a rule they are tuned to note 6 and the 2 below it (*pelog* or *slendro*), though for pieces in *pelog pathet lima* (explained in the next chapter) both are lowered by one note, giving 5 and 1. In fact, what appear to be two strings really comprise a single length of wire wound around the bottom of the stick and ending in the two pegs. The bow is as ornate and fragile as the *rebab* itself. It is held, palm upwards, in such a way that the third and fourth fingers pull the hair, thereby giving it the required tension. The *rebab* is held vertically, or slightly tilting forwards, in front of the player. The fingers press the strings lightly; there is no fingerboard and no attempt is made to press them against the neck. Nevertheless, the instrument is capable of making a fairly loud, nasal sound. To soften and sweeten it various devices may be used. One is to tie the strings together with cotton an inch or so below the bridge and pinch a rolled leaf between them and the bridge; another is to wedge a piece of cloth between the strings and the lower part of the skin cover.

The *kendhang* typically consists of three or four drums, all of similar barrel shape with a skin (from goat or buffalo) at each end and thongs connecting them which may be tightened by small rings (to the shape of the letter 'Y') or slackened (to the shape of the letter 'V'). The drums are of very different sizes, from the large *kendhang gendhing* or *ageng* to the small *kendhang ketipung*. The *kendhang gendhing* and the middle-sized *kendhang ciblon* (sometimes called *kendhang batangan*) and the *kendhang wayangan* are cradled in small stands, while the *ketipung* is held in the lap or rested on the floor. In each case the larger head (giving the lower sounds) of the drum is to the player's *right*, and all the playing is done using the hands alone.[2] The technique required for the *kendhang gendhing* and *ketipung* is relatively simple, as there are only about half a dozen strokes and the rhythms are uncomplicated. The *ciblon* and *kendhang wayangan*, however, are much harder to play since they have a varied range of sounds, many of which are difficult to master, and faster patterns which rely, moreover, on a subtle use of rubato. The *kendhang wayangan* is slightly larger than the *ciblon*, and is used to accompany the *wayang* shadow play. The *ciblon* is used to accompany dance, and also in concert pieces, borrowing patterns from the dance music. For this reason, the large gamelans destined primarily for concert music, may well dispense with a *kendhang wayangan*, and in any case the *ciblon* may be used to accompany *wayang* if necessary. The origin and essence of the distinctive *ciblon* style, which sounds much livelier than the somewhat reticent patterns of the other drums, is in the name itself, which means 'splashing in water'. It is typical of the Javanese that they should have devised a musically ingenious and intricate game by slapping the surface of water in complex multi-rhythmic patterns. Many of the sounds of the *ciblon* drum have just this slapping quality and an almost mischievous exuberance. Kunst, who draws attention to this link between music and play, writes: 'It is as if, in the hands of an essentially musical race such as the Javanese, everything is turned into music.'[3] We may add here that clapping the hands together (having the wonderfully onomatopoeic name *keplok*) in interlocking patterns is also an important accompaniment to gamelan music of the lively variety, usually in conjunction with the *ciblon* drum. These observations should also help guard against the view often held by Westerners in respect of the gamelan, and oriental culture in general, that it is an unchanging, sacrosanct tradition. 'High art' usually owes far more to 'folk art' than is acknowledged, and in the case of gamelan a rigid distinction between these categories has little value anyway.

Many complete gamelans possess a large barrel-shaped drum called *bedhug*, which is suspended from above in a frame. The heads are of equal size and nailed, and one of the heads is struck with a beater. Because of the strong thud produced, the drum is restricted to certain loud pieces, usually associated with dance or ceremonial occasions.

The *gambang* has already been mentioned as a *wilah* instrument but the *wilah* are made of wood rather than bronze, hence the full name of the instrument: *gambang kayu* (*kayu* = wood). A *gambang gangsa* (bronze *gambang*), looking like a multi-octave *saron*, used to be found in the gamelan but nowadays it is virtually obsolete. Kunst[4] suggests that this archaic instrument may be the prototype of the entire *saron* group, on a single instrument. The wood used for the normal *gambang wilah* must be very hard, and a type known as *berlian* is favoured for this purpose. The *rancak* is a common trough resonator, like that of the *saron* group, but much deeper and with thinner sides and a relatively narrow slit aperture at the top. The *wilah*, secured in the same way as on the *saron* group but with much thinner pins, are also much longer, from about 58 cm to 29 cm. (The length decreases as the pitch rises.) The number of *wilah* may vary but the typical arrangement is nineteen in *pelog* (from low 6 to high 3) and twenty in *slendro* (from low 6 to high 5). In *pelog* the scale uses either note 1 or 7. The change-over can be effected quickly and obviate the need for a second *pelog rancak* and duplication of *wilah*. The mallets have very long handles (about 35 cm or so). They are made of thin and flexible buffalo horn ending in a wooden disc surrounded by a felt ring, as on the *gender* mallets. Two mallets are used and the *gambang* part is usually among the fastest in the gamelan, providing a gentle, rippling sound quite unlike the harsher effects of the Western orchestral xylophone. Because no damping is required and also because the part is in parallel octaves for most of the time, the *gambang* is easier to play than the *gender*. The only problem with playing in octaves is that the *wilah* (and the octave gap) narrow considerably as the pitch rises, and it is therefore all too easy for the inexperienced player to hit a large number of wrong notes.

The *siter* and larger *celempung* also play elaborations of the melody, in the case of the *siter* not unlike those of the *gambang* but even closer to those of the *gender panerus*. Indeed, it is acceptable to transfer the entire *gender panerus* part to the *siter*. The word *siter* is from the Dutch 'cither', hence English 'zither', which basically describes the instrument: an oblong box resonator with plucked, tunable strings. A common

41

model has eleven or twelve pairs of unison strings, spanning the range from low 2 or 3 to the high 3 two octaves above, on each side of the box. The difference is that one side is in *slendro* and the instrument is turned over to give the *pelog* notes (which follow the scale patterns found on the *gender*s and *gambang*, but in this case the change of scale can be done on the spot, using a small key). The *celempung* is a larger version on ornate legs (and thus cannot be turned over, necessitating two or three *celempung*s in a complete gamelan). The sound, especially of the more popular *siter*, cuts through the gamelan texture and can easily assume an unwarranted, even slightly incongruous, prominence.

This problem of balance similarly affects the remaining instruments to be discussed, including the human voice, but a major difference is that their parts are either intermittent or are actually required to stand out, or both. The *suling* is a simple bamboo end-blown flute, with a notch cut into the side of the (stopped) top end which is surrounded by a ratan or bamboo ring, leaving a small slit. There are five finger-holes on the *pelog* instrument and four on the *slendro* one. The *pelog suling* is approximately 57.5 cm long, while the *slendro* is approximately 53 cm. Techniques of over-blowing, cross-fingering and half-holing permit this, the simplest and cheapest instrument in the gamelan, to provide one of the most exquisite, expressive and fluid lines in the ensemble. Because of this potential, it may be grouped with the *rebab* and the voice, but its part is freer and comes in short, disjointed phrases rather than as a continuous line, which distinguishes it from all the other embellishing instruments.

The *keprak* is one of many instruments that may be used in the gamelan for special, limited purposes. It is a simple box or slit drum, essentially a small block of wood with a resonant hollow and slit along the top, which is struck with a small wooden hammer. It is used in various dance performances as a signal to the dancers, and for this reason its sound is obtrusive yet sporadic.

Although the human voice is left until the end of this section, most cultures regard it as the foremost musical instrument. There is even some justification for treating it as such in the context of Javanese gamelan, where its status has risen dramatically in recent times. More important than this, however, is the concept of an inner melody which is the common basis of all the parts in the gamelan and yet which is not stated literally by any instrument. Rather, it is in the minds of the musicians. It is therefore felt, or, one may say, internally *sung*. The 'external' vocal parts in the gamelan are further strands in the polyphony, on a par with the embellishments of the instruments, rather than any attempt to manifest this inner melody. Two main types may be distinguished: the *sindhen* (or *sindhenan*), for solo female voice, and the *gerongan*, for a chorus of three or four men. It is common to have more than one *pesindhen* (woman who sings the *sindhen*) in a piece but the women will sing in turn rather than as a group. Another important feature is that the women sit near the front, or even in front, of the gamelan and nowadays very often have a microphone. In most cases they are the only members of the ensemble to have such amplification, and even when a recording is being made, necessitating the use of microphones throughout the gamelan, the levels tend to be set in favour of the *sindhen*. Moreover, the *pesindhen* is often the only performer to be named. Perhaps this prominence may be explained by the fact that she is likely to be the only woman in the ensemble. The *gender* player in *wayang kulit* is often the wife or mother of the *dhalang*, but this is not imperative, and the player is just as likely to be a man. Although the prominence of the *pesindhen* is a fact of modern gamelan life, many deplore this departure from the musical equality which is one of the main attributes of the ensemble.

The *sindhen* may be compared with the parts for *rebab* and *suling* in its rhythmic elasticity and wealth of ornamentation. It is, however, more continuous than the *suling* line and more ornate than the *rebab* melody. The singer's tone is not unlike that of the *rebab*, but – in this writer's opinion – is even closer to an oboe than any stringed instrument.

The *gerongan* is a much simpler melody, in terms of rhythm and ornamentation, and it is often included with the *balungan* in printed notations of gamelan compositions. It is usually confined to one section of the whole piece. A typical example is *Ladrang Wilujeng*, discussed in Chapter 5, where the *gerongan* occurs only in the second section (whereas the *sindhen* continues throughout the piece).

These two vocal genres may be found in most large-scale gamelan compositions (thus it can be said that most Javanese gamelan music nowadays uses the human voice) but they are by no means the only ones. Among the others may be mentioned *bawa*, a male solo with discreet support on the *gender*, which is often used to introduce large

43

compositions, and the chorus, similar to *gerongan* but in fact called *sindhen*, which is sung by women and men in unison to accompany the court dances *bedhaya* and *serimpi*.

The complete gamelan is laid out according to certain conventions, for example the largest gongs are at the back, the *balungan* instruments in the centre, and the embellishing instruments at the front. The audience would probably be facing the front in rather formal concert situations, but they are often free to sit at the sides or behind and to wander around.

Gamelan manufacture and tuning: the story of Gamelan Sekar Pethak

The preceding section on the instruments of the gamelan focused on the examples comprising Gamelan Sekar Pethak. The following account of how the instruments are made and tuned rests almost entirely on my observations of the manufacture and tuning of that gamelan between September and November 1981. The background to this research sheds some light on the recent history of gamelan manufacture in Java. Kunst, who gave an account of the situation before Indonesian Independence, struck a very pessimistic note, stating the craft to be 'on the verge of ruin' and noting the decline, even demise, of the Semarang gong-smithies, going on to warn of the complete extinction of the craft 'unless, in some way or other, a helping hand is offered in the nick of time'.[5] It would appear that Kunst's warning was heeded by his own pupil Mantle Hood who encouraged Reso Wiguno in the village of Wirun near Solo to revitalize his manufacture of gamelan instruments in the 1950s. Another American, John Pemberton (a friend and fellow player with me in the Wesleyan University gamelan) became closely involved during the early 1970s with Tentrem Sarwanto (born 1940) working in Semanggi on the outskirts of Solo, and actually learnt some of the skills involved in making and tuning gamelan instruments. I was introduced to Pak Tentrem in 1977 by another Wesleyan graduate student, Alex Dea, and commissioned a *slendro saron* and *slenthem* with the limited funds available. Time did not permit collection of the instruments nor funds their dispatch to England, so they remained in Solo. My next trip to Java did not occur until August 1981, when the

44

University of York made enough funds available for the purchase of a complete gamelan. It is generally accepted that an old gamelan is preferable to a new one, assuming it has been maintained in good condition; for one thing the tuning has stabilized, and it is widely maintained that the quality of the bronze and workmanship are better. A few weeks of hunting in the regions of Solo and Jogja (and even as far away as Jakarta) convinced me that the older gamelans were either in poor condition and incomplete or, if not, then far beyond my budget (of around £8,000). As a feeling of despair was setting in, I chanced to meet another American gamelan player, Barry Drummond, who informed me that, by a remarkable coincidence, he had that very day visited Pak Tentrem, who had raised the problem of what to do with the two instruments for which someone from England had paid four years earlier but left behind. If nothing else, this suggested an extraordinary degree of honesty and patience, and I eagerly accepted Barry's advice that I should go and discuss the project of a complete gamelan with Pak Tentrem.

Apart from the very reasonable quotation, which was well within my budget, there were two other clear and irresistible advantages in commissioning Pak Tentrem to make the entire set. One was that it would encourage the continuation of a great skill and the other was that it would enable me to to witness the birth of a complete gamelan. This extraordinary process, in which the instruments are beaten and filed, rather than cast into the final shape, and without the aid of any machinery other than a couple of very simple devices, remains one of the greatest wonders in the world of musical instrument-making. To see a gong slowly taking shape from a small black disc through patient and skilled hammering is truly an amazing experience, verging on an optical illusion!

Work commenced around 10 September (1981) and reached its climax on 22 November, when the gamelan was played for the first time. The season was ideal, remaining mostly dry. Forging during the rainy season is hazardous, since the water can easily come through the roof on to the hot bronze, thereby breaking it. Pak Tentrem told me that one *kenong* had suffered this fate during a freak shower but that had been the only such problem. The one advantage of the rainy season is that the lower temperatures are better for tuning the instruments.

In order to create the whole gamelan in such a short space of time,

Pak Tentrem employed about ten men (the number was not constant), working on average eight hours a day, six days a week. This was just for the bronze parts; the wooden cases, mallets, resonators and accessories were made at other workshops in Solo. The large *gong ageng* was made across the Solo river at Pak Reso Wiguno's famous smithy in the village of Wirun, because Pak Tentrem's place was not big enough for this one instrument.

The tools and other paraphernalia for making the bronze instruments will be briefly described before proceeding to an account of the work itself. It must be stressed that this is the writing of a layman, based on observation and discussion with Pak Tentrem. More detailed scientific publications devoted entirely to this craft appear to be very rare.[6] The hut of the smithy itself is called *besalen*; the one used by Pak Tentrem adjoined his own living quarters and was no larger than his living room. For this reason only half a dozen men could work in it at a time. Dug into the ground near the centre of the hut is a space for the charcoal fire (*prapen*), and directly above it a hole is cut in the roof. A pipe connects the fire with a bellows (*lamus*) in the form of a leather bag. At about a similar distance from the fire and approximately at right angles are the anvils, called *tandhes*, which are sunk in the ground and made of iron for *wilah* and stone for *pencon*. There are also small concavities of various sizes into which the central knobs of the *pencon* are beaten and shaped. In a corner of the *besalen* is a water bath, called *pelandhan*, which is also usually sunk in the ground. These are the fixed items; the remaining tools and accessories are portable. Several clay cups (*kowi*), used for melting the metals, are stacked in a corner. Near them are the moulds, called *penyingen*, which are of two main kinds: one for the *wilah* (oblong) shape and the other for the *pencon* (circular) shape. Apart from the various tongs used for manipulating and carrying the hot metal, the most important tools used in the forging process are the hammers, called *palu*. There are about a dozen kinds, varying in shape and weight (up to about 8 kilos), but the unusual feature common to most of them is the long head, which is about the same length as the handle. In most cases the head is made of iron and the handle of wood, but one or two particularly large specimens are made entirely of wood. Other accessories in the *besalen* include scales to weigh the copper and tin, long tapers to light the interior of the *pencon* (the inside of the *besalen* is very dark and without electricity), gauges to check the

Peking

Saron

Demung

Slenthem

Gender

Gongs (Ageng and Suwukan) and Kempuls

Kenong

Kethuk and Kempyang

Bonang

Rebab

Gambang

Siter

Suling

Kecer

ree Kendhangs (playing Ciblon)

Kemanak

Gong Kemodhong

uniform diameter of *pencon*, and pieces of matting and banana leaf as protection from the heat.

The extensive hammering necessary to fashion instruments particularly of the *pencon* type is first done on the hot bronze, inside the *besalen*, using the *prapen*, and then mainly outdoors, on the cold bronze, which by then has assumed the final shape of the instrument. For part of the process a curious contraption called *entol* is used, consisting of a long pole, one end of which slots into a tree or specially constructed post. At about a third of its length from the tree is fixed a short wooden pole, called *umbul*, which points perpendicularly from the *entol* to the ground. At the far end of the *entol* sit three or four men, as though on a see-saw, and their weight is used to press the *umbul* firmly downwards. The larger gongs are placed *pencu* downwards and resting in a wooden concavity and the *umbul* presses down on the inside of the gong at carefully determined points between the *pencu* and the edge. Cold hammering on either side of the *umbul* is then carried out, using small hammers with short heads of the familiar type. The purpose of this work is to even out the shape of the gong and ensure a uniform surface. A shorter *umbul* is used for hammering on the outside of the gong, since the inverted gong rests higher from the ground.

The filing is also done outside. It can be an even lengthier process than the hammering since it is usually performed by one man at a time, using a variety of files called *kikir*, from a very coarse, banana-shaped implement (*kikir patar*) to one which is no more than a curved knife-blade (*kikir kesik*). This, and various emery cloths, are used for the final stages. A simple manual lathe, called *alat bubut*, (perhaps the nearest thing to a machine in the entire process) is used to cut a groove (*tikel*) around the base of the *pencu*. Drills are used to bore holes in the larger gongs (which are hung in the gamelan) and all *wilah*.

The main stages in the manufacture of a bronze gamelan idiophone are:

1 Mixing the bronze
The best kind of metal is a kind of bronze known as *gangsa* which is distinguished by its higher than normal tin component: the correct ratio of copper (*tembaga*) to tin (*rejasa*) is 10:3. According to some, including Pak Tentrem, it is the last syllables of the two words which give the name to this special alloy. *Gangsa* is also the word in high Javanese for

gamelan, so the everyday Indonesian word for bronze (*perunggu*) is commonly used to avoid this confusion. The maker buys the metals separately, then weighs and mixes them himself. (Pak Tentrem told me that less scrupulous makers reduce the expensive tin content.) Two small pieces of bronze are made for testing. One is left to cool and then broken with a hammer. The other is hammered while still hot and should not break, but tolerate hammering until it is really thin. The inner surface of the broken piece is examined: if it is too rough, tin must be added, if too smooth, copper must be added. The tin is not only a smoothing agent but helps to give a superior sound, as well as a relatively light colour to the bronze.

2 *Forging*

The accepted bronze is poured into a mould. The moulds (*penyingen*) are of different sizes but of two basic shapes: one for *wilah* and the other for *pencon*. The *wilah* emerge from the mould in the oblong shape which is very close to the final shape, whereas the *pencon* emerge as discs, with one surface flat and the other convex. The hammering is a lengthy process – up to two hours for a small *pencon* or *wilah* and at least two days for the largest *gong* – and requires up to four men. In the case of the larger *pencon*, which start as small discs and end as gongs with no equal in the world, the process, repeated over and over again until the desired shape is almost miraculously achieved, relies on the meticulously co-ordinated functions of a group of craftsmen. One man (*panji*)[7] turns the metal in the charcoal fire (*prapen*) activated by the hand-operated bellows (*lamus*), requiring one or two men (*pelamus*). Another (*pengalap*) caries the red-hot metal from the fire to the sunken anvil (*tandhes*). While the metal is turned by one man (*pengider*) the hammerers (from one to four, depending on the stage in the process, and having various names, such as *pengarep*, *penengah*, *penepong*, and *pengapit*, according to their function) work in perfect co-ordination for around a quarter to half a minute, before the metal has cooled too much and has to be returned to the fire. (It should be noted that most of the workers appeared to exchange jobs quite freely – a nice parallel between making a gamelan and playing it.) Hammering usually begins in a circle near the centre of the disc, and then gradually moves towards the edge.

No less exciting than the sight of this extraordinary and ancient craft is the sound. Anyone with the slightest musical curiosity cannot fail to notice the variety of dramatic sounds which the work produces. The *palu* with the long, iron heads, used to forge *pencon*, emit different pitches as they strike the hot bronze, so that the rhythmic hammering sounds a little like high-pitched, staccato bell-ringing. 'Gamelan music' therefore begins before the instruments have even come into existence! At the end of the whole process the instrument is quenched in the bath (*pelandhan*), and this immersion of hot metal in cool water produces a short but dramatic roar. The larger the instrument the more dramatic the roar. So, in the case of the largest gong, in which so much time and expertise have been invested, the climactic roar, which announces literally a 'make-or-break situation', is every bit as crucial as any sound the gong is destined to make as the most important instrument in the gamelan.

By the time it is finally quenched the item being forged will already give a clear note, but above the desired pitch to allow for the lowering of pitch that will occur during the filing stage. The maker will have calculated this, allowing for the fact that the larger the instrument, the higher it should be above the target pitch during forging. In the case of the large gongs, further hammering must be done on the cold metal to even out the shape.

3 Filing

At this stage the bronze is still *cemengan* (from the high Javanese word for black) meaning that it is not only black but rough. Very often the *gong ageng* is left in this state except for the *pencu*, which is smoothed. (The *cemengan* state, with the many marks from the hammer blows, can be seen on the inside of all *pencon* instruments of the gamelan.) The filing and sandpapering can take about twice as long as the forging. At the end the bronze has its smoothness and beautiful colour, and is nearly in tune, but fine tuning is done when everything is finished and the whole gamelan can be tuned together.

4 Tuning

It is relatively easy to grasp the theory of gamelan tuning, but very hazardous to put it into practice. *Wilah* and *bumbung* (resonators) are fairly easy to tune but *pencon* require hammering and only an expert should undertake this to minimize the risk of cracking or breaking. The question of what to tune to (since there is no standardization of pitch or intervallic structure in Java) is answered by the maker in consultation with the purchaser. It appears to be common practice to copy the tuning of some well-known gamelan; in Solo the favourites are those at the radio station (RRI) and the famous Gamelan Kyai Kanyut Mesem at the Mangkunegaran Palace. Such a model is called the *babon*, which literally means the 'mother hen'. This practice of copying has been criticized for the good reason that it could lead to standardization. For a set destined for export to what was then virtually 'Das Land ohne Gamelan' this was not a real problem, and Gamelan Sekar Pethak was loosely modelled on the RRI gamelan. The maker will usually begin by making a few *wilah* (*gender barung* and perhaps *gambang*) tuned to the *babon*. The rest of the gamelan is tuned together when the forging has been completed, using these *wilah* as a reference.

The pitch of *wilah* is lowered by filing the underneath near the middle (between the holes) and raised by filing the underneath near each end. On the thin *wilah blimbingan* the work may be done on the top of the key if the underneath has already been filed too much. The *bumbung* (tube resonators for the *genders* and *slenthem*) have either a wide or narrow aperture at the top. Both types can be partially closed with sticky tape to lower the pitch. The narrow type of aperture can be enlarged by filing to raise the pitch, whereas in the wide type wax or sometimes sand is poured in to raise the pitch. This stage is straightforward and mistakes can easily be rectified.

As has already been noted, the technique of tuning *pencon* is very difficult, though the principles may be simply expressed. Before the work can begin, the craftsman must determine which areas of the gong are thick and which are thin. This is done by feeling the vibrations with the fingers. With the more raised *pencon pangkon* type, and also the *kethuk*, the area near the *pencu* on the outside is hammered to lower the pitch, and the area opposite on the inside is hammered to raise the pitch. On the larger, flatter *pencon gandhul* the same area on the outside is hammered to lower the pitch but to raise it the hammering on the inside is done nearer the rim. The bronze must be supported by iron or wood directly below the area of hammering in all cases, and the *pencu* is never hammered. Various methods, such as loading the gong at strategic points with wax, or even pouring water in, are commonly used by those who are unqualified and therefore unwilling to attempt the hammering, and a judicious amount of filing can also be undertaken. The area which is hammered on the raised *pencon pangkon* and *kethuk* to lower the pitch may be filed instead. To raise the pitch, however, the top of the *pencu* is filed. On the larger *pencon gandhul* a certain amount of filing can be done in conjunction with hammering to lower the pitch. In general, the *pencon gandhul* instruments are by far the hardest to tune, because the sound must first be focused (*kempel*). This is usually done by applying clay to various parts of the gong to determine which parts must be hammered. The problem is that the subsequent hammering for tuning unfocuses the sound, so the process has to be repeated until the sound is both focused and in tune.

This information on manufacture and tuning came mostly from one maker (Pak Tentrem) and does not necessarily accord in all details and terminology with other accounts. An interesting comparison may be made with Kunst's description of the craft half a century ago.[8] Much of the terminology is different but the essential procedures are the same and have doubtless remained so for centuries. It would appear that as the art of forging bronze instruments declined during Kunst's time, so the simpler skill of making gamelan idiophones from iron, which is of course much cheaper than bronze, flourished. The rebirth of bronze-working in the last thirty years has not supplanted this alternative. The best iron gamelans sound nearly as good as bronze ones, even if no amount of gold paint can make them look as beautiful, and are popular in the villages and among the less prosperous in general. Pak Tentrem's own work in bronze appeared to be fairly piecemeal. In fact, he told me that Gamelan Sekar Pethak was his first commission for a complete *pelog* and *slendro* gamelan. Otherwise he would be kept busy making additional or replacement instruments for existing sets or repairing old instruments, with his excellent products travelling as far afield as Japan and America, as well as within Java itself.

The ceremony to inaugurate and name Gamelan Sekar Pethak, as well as to play it for the first time, took place on 22 November 1981. Crammed into the main room of a house adjoining Pak Tentrem's were the instruments and a cosmopolitan group of musicians. Ten were Javanese professional gamelan players, mostly from the radio station and the two Solonese courts, and there were six American students and one Australian, all advanced in the art of gamelan playing. (The one European was occupied recording the whole event!) It was appropriate that this gamelan, destined for a group of Western musicians, should be inaugurated in a way that reflects the global impact of the gamelan. The impromptu concert also allowed Pak Tentrem to listen critically to the complete set and – in the ensuing days before everything was packed and transported to Jogja and thence to Jakarta – to make a few minor adjustments. This could only be a preliminary measure, however, because a new gamelan must be 'played in' for a few years, as frequently and vigorously as possible, with occasional tuning, until the bronze has settled and the tuning stabilized. In the early years of a gamelan's existence lower pitches will tend to rise more than higher ones, and the manufacturer can check this to some extent by tuning the larger instruments slightly below pitch.

The inaugural ceremony was marked by typically Javanese informality, with crowds of children among those filling the doorways and other available space, giving free voice to their interest in this unusual spectacle. There was also a ceremonial aspect, in the form of offerings of flowers, fruit and incense beneath the *gong ageng*. The gamelan also assumed its name, an optional nicety which is essential only in the case of old and respected palace gamelans. It is a mistake to think of all gamelans as being sacred and enshrouded in mystical beliefs and rituals. The only instance which suggested something of the kind during the entire manufacture of this gamelan was when Pak Reso Wiguno (whose smithy was borrowed to make the *gong ageng*) refused to start the work on the day called *Sabtu-Kliwon* (Saturday 31 October, *Sabtu*, Saturday, coinciding with *Kliwon* of the Javanese five-day week) because this is regarded as a *Hari Kramat*, a holy day with supernatural associations. (It will be noted that it was Halloween: our closest example of a *Hari Kramat*.) Even here, however, I was warned against reading too much into the situation. As for naming the gamelan, if I had not made the suggestion it is quite clear that the question would not have arisen. Pak Tentrem told me he did not regard it as necessary, nor did he and his men perform any rituals which are supposedly traditional in gamelan making. It is only because the gamelan was destined for York, which is always identified by the emblem of a white rose, that this typically fragrant name for a gamelan was chosen. My initial translation of white rose into Indonesian and low Javanese was *Mawar Putih* (the name always used by its maker, when he remembered it at all), but Professor James T. Siegel (in Solo at that time) indicated that a high Javanese name would be more respectful.[9] He accordingly suggested Sekar Pethak. The latter word still means white, but the former is especially rich in meanings, including flower. It occurs in the names of several old gamelans and can refer to the music itself, especially to kinds of vocal music. The name, enshrining music and the white flower, was therefore considered ideal for this particular gamelan.

Since it arrived at York in April 1982, Gamelan Sekar Pethak has been used extensively in classes and regular rehearsals within the university music department, and has made several concert and workshop appearances around England and Scotland (also Italy), including one at the 1982 Henry Wood Promenade Concerts, when it was played by the Sasono Mulyo group from Solo. It has also been used for a number of educational projects with school and college students. This wider context and application is typical of gamelan as a modern world music.

Notes

1 These and subsequent measurements are based on Gamelan Sekar Pethak, and are included as a general guide to the dimensions of the instruments, without discounting the possibility of wide variations in other sets.
2 Kunst, op. cit., p. 203, noted that in villages, the drums were often held the other way round (which is still common today) conforming to the usual association of low pitches with the left, and high with the right, which applies to the other instruments of the gamelan.
3 Ibid., p. 294.
4 Ibid., p. 171.
5 Ibid., p. 140.
6 Three are included here, rather than in the bibliography, because none is easily obtainable and the most detailed one in English (the first on the list) is probably the hardest to find:
    Be acquainted with the gamelan and its manufacture (a guide book for the participants of ASEAN workshop on the manufacture of the Indonesian gamelan, Solo, Indonesia, 26 March–1 April 1981). Manuscript compiled in Jakarta, 1981;
    Jacobson, Edward, and Van Hasselt, J. H. *De Gong-Fabricatie te Semarang* (Leiden, E. J. Brill, 1907). Translated by Andrew Toth, *The Manufacture of Gongs in Semarang, (Indonesia* 19, 1975), pp. 127–72, Modern Indonesia Project, Cornell University;
    Rustopo *Pengetahuan membuat gamelan* (Knowledge of making gamelan), Proyek Pengembangan IKI sub Bagian Proyek ASKI Surakarta 1980/1981.
    I should also mention that Sam Quigley, of the Boston Museum of Fine Arts, and a Director of the expert Boston Village Gamelan, has recently (1989) produced a video of gong-making at Pak Tentrem's smithy. At the time of going to press, the tape had not been seen by the author, but copies are available from Sam Quigley.

7 This name is taken from the Javanese epic of the Prince Panji. Kunst, op. cit., pp. 137–8, remarks on the use by gamelan makers of names from this epic as a means of disguising their everyday identity and protecting themselves from the evil spirits which might attend the manufacturing process.

8 Ibid., pp. 136–41.

9 Ben Arps (personal communication, 1989) disputes this, pointing out that low Javanese and the archaic form (*kawi*) are preferred to the high form (*krama*) in naming gamelans. It is not so much that we have ended up with a wrong name for this gamelan as that it still might not be the most likely. Had Ben advised me in November 1981, the set would probably be called Gamelan Kembang Seta, or Gamelan Puspa Seta. My reaction is the more names the better, so we could add these two to the two (Sekar Pethak and Mawar Putih) already in use.

Chapter 4

Rudiments of *Karawitan*

Karawitan (literally 'refinement') is broadly synonymous with gamelan music, in other words it is the conceptual framework and theoretical content of the *gendhing* (gamelan composition). Strictly speaking it is music, be it instrumental or vocal, in either of the traditional Javanese tuning systems, and the gamelan music of today, blending instrumental and vocal parts within these two tuning systems, is the fullest and most typical example of *karawitan*. The subject does not yield its deepest secrets willingly, and the Javanese themselves are exercised by some of its knottier problems. Here we must try and steer round such obstacles, without underestimating the depth and complexity. A knowledge of the basics of *karawitan* is essential, and the aim here is to keep it as clear and simple as possible. There are many ways of dividing the subject; the ordering and priority of elements which follow do not pretend to be definitive, and much has had to be omitted or treated briefly. There should, however, be enough to provide an introduction and basis for the understanding of the next chapter, which is *karawitan* in practice.

1 *Laras*

The main condition for *karawitan* is that it is in one of the two Javanese tuning systems, or *laras*. Although a complete Javanese gamelan is regarded as a unit, it is usually two gamelans placed together, one for each *laras*, with most of the corresponding instruments placed adjacently at right angles, and this contributes to the impression of one large gamelan. The two *laras* are called *slendro* and *pelog*, and it is quite simply because the tuning of the gamelan cannot be altered in performance that it is necessary to build complete sets in each *laras*. A gamelan in only one of the two *laras*, called *gamelan sepangkon*, must not be thought of as incomplete, though of course to play the repertoire of both *slendro* and *pelog* pieces it is necessary to have the kind of double gamelan, called *gamelan seprangkat*, which has already been described as typical.

The basic information about *laras* is easy to grasp, and it should never be a problem to distinguish one from the other. *Slendro* is defined as an anhemitonic pentatonic scale. This means it has five notes and no semitones, which would also describe the scale obtained on the black notes of the piano. The crucial difference is that the five notes of *slendro* are more or less equally spaced, while the black notes have clear differences between whole tones and minor thirds. The problem for the Western ear is relating the pitches of such a subdivision. Divisions of the octave into twelve equal intervals (semitones), six (whole tones), four (minor thirds: the diminished seventh chord), three (major thirds: the augmented triad) and two (tritones) are familiar, but the 'missing' division between one and six is not used in Western music, and this is the territory of *slendro*. If the octave is divided into five equal parts, the resultant interval will lie between a whole tone and a minor third. The somewhat elusive quality of *slendro* is that we cannot say exactly where, because in practice the octave is not divided into five precisely equal steps. The Western love of standardization means that such a situation could be regarded as unsatisfactory, but the Javanese attach great importance to *embat*, or intervallic structure. Much of a gamelan's unique personality depends on its *embat*, and a good ear will appreciate the subtle differences between the notes of *slendro* or *pelog* from one gamelan to another.

Pelog is readily distinguished from *slendro*. For one thing it has seven available notes (though in a great number of pieces not all seven will be used) and for another the size of interval varies far more than in *slendro* and includes semitones. Having emphasized the variability and desirability of *embat* we may give a typical – necessarily approximate – representation of the two *laras*. This could be done on a grid, showing relationships to fixed intervals and notes, but this would immediately suggest something precise, and the intention here is only to give a visual impression of the two *laras* in relation to each other. In order to give an idea of the kinds of intervals, without being too specific, the two *laras* are shown from a low 6 to just beyond the 6 an octave above (and of course the two notes 1 in *slendro* and 7 in *pelog* also span one octave). Note that in the cipher notation system the number 4 is omitted in *slendro*. (This is to facilitate direct comparison between the names and functions of the notes in the two *laras*.)

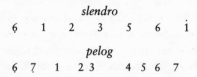

In this admittedly free scheme one important decision had to be made. Although *slendro* and *pelog* are independent and not played simultaneously, they must nevertheless coincide at some predetermined point in a *gamelan seprangkat* to permit effective transitions from one *laras* to the other. There must, therefore, be a note common to both *laras*. The Javanese call it the exchange or coinciding note: *tumbuk*. Another nice avoidance of standardization is that not all *gamelan (seprangkat)* have the same *tumbuk* note, let alone the same *embat*. Nowadays it must be said that the majority have *tumbuk nem* – note 6 as identical in *slendro* and *pelog* – though several have *tumbuk lima* (meeting on note five). In a *tumbuk nem* gamelan there is likely to be a secondary coincidence of note 5 in *slendro* with note 4 in *pelog*. The above scheme, representing a *tumbuk nem* gamelan, shows this, as well of course as the alignment of the two notes 6.[1]

2 *Pathet*

The pitch material of even *slendro* and *pelog* together may strike the Westerner as limited, but this is to miss a very important point about oriental music, even music throughout the whole world. The greatest refinement and artistry can be demonstrated with the smallest amount of material; the limitations discipline the mind, which in turn strives to transcend these limits, and from this beneficial friction are created the pearls of the music. In India five notes are sufficient for a *raga*, on which a good musician can improvise for hours without feeling any need whatsoever to add any notes. Furthermore, several different *raga*s may have exactly the same notes and yet be readily distinguishable. This subtlety is matched in *karawitan*, where the five notes of *slendro* may be arranged in different ways, the same applying to *pelog*; and this is the basis of the concept of *pathet*.

Even in Western music we can find a crude analogy that may help illuminate this difficult topic. Just with the five black notes of the keyboard, for example, five different tonalities can be established, or at least implied. Without recourse to harmonic devices (perfect cadences and the like) this can be done melodically by altering the hierarchy of the notes, probably by bringing out the tonic and dominant of the tonality in question and relatively underplaying other notes which may challenge this relationship. This is, at the simplest level, how *pathet* works, but the subject becomes far more complex, and whole treatises are written on it alone. Perhaps no other aspect of *karawitan* exercises the mind as much as *pathet*, and even the most expert of Javanese masters approach it with caution and utmost respect. Martopangrawit prefaces his account with the following remarks:

> What is pathet? This question is always on my mind. I think no definition has yet been satisfactory, due to the fact that the word 'pathet' has so many different uses, and each use fulfills a particular need. So if one is to offer an explanation of pathet, the explanation must be relevant to the particular need at hand. For example, I once asked an ironsmith, 'What is a knife?' He answered, 'A knife is a kind of machete, but smaller.' It is understandable that his definition had to do with the shape of the object, since as a toolmaker and vendor, he assumed that the questioner was a prospective customer and would want to calculate the cost of the object. However, when I asked a noodle vendor the same question, I got a very different answer. He said that a knife is an instrument used to cut onions, cabbage, and the like, while a machete is an instrument used to split wood. He wanted to impress upon the customer that he was a man who kept things clean and would not mix dirty and clean implements.[2]

We must therefore attempt an account of *pathet* appropriate to this book. As has already been adumbrated, it is a kind of melodic tonality operating within the two *laras*, and there are three *pathet*s in each. (Sometimes a fourth *pathet* in *pelog*, called *pelog pathet manyura* or *nyamat*, is found, but it is much rarer than the other three.) *Pathet* means 'constraint' or 'limit', which is very much in keeping with the aesthetics of Javanese and other oriental musics already discussed. The five notes of *slendro* are raw material, and do not take on shape and beauty until they are organized into a *pathet*. The same applies to *pelog*, where the situation is somewhat complicated by the fact that all seven notes seem too many for a *pathet*, and the pentatonic basis of *slendro* influences this *laras*. Of course, this can prove an advantage, since if exactly the same five notes must be used in *slendro* for each *pathet*, making it hard for the untrained ear to distinguish one from another, in *pelog* different sets of five main notes can be extracted from the available seven, making the task easier.

The three *pathet*s of *slendro* are called *pathet nem*, *pathet sanga*, and *pathet manyura*; those of *pelog* are called *pathet lima*, *pathet nem*, and *pathet barang*. One of the mysteries of the subject is how these names came about. *Lima* and *nem* mean five and six respectively and can refer to actual notes, but the connection is not clear. *Sanga*, meaning nine, is still less clear. *Barang* ('thing') can refer to note 7 in *pelog*, which is useful since this *pelog pathet* is broadly distinguished from the other two by its prominent use of that note, but the significance of *manyura* (derived from the Sanskrit word for peacock) remains tantalizing.

Attempts are made to isolate the *pathet* from the material played by certain instruments in the gamelan. For example, if the *balungan* is considered to be the nuclear melody, the 'cantus firmus', to which everything relates, then it is logical to expect it to reveal the *pathet*. But this overlooks a far more important priority: the reality of the music is only expressed by the complete ensemble, and every contribution should be considered. In practice, the Javanese are likely to prefer the *gender* to the *saron* or other *balungan* instrument if only one of them is to be chosen, and they will probably stress the vocal applications – even the very origin – of *pathet*. Indeed, an important part of a gamelan performance and of *wayang* is the use of short preludes and postludes collectively called *pathetan*. The name indicates their importance in establishing and confirming the *pathet*, and the way they are performed underlines the importance of the voice (which leads in the *wayang*), and of the *rebab*, *gender*, *gambang* and *suling* which follow the melodic line in a free rhythm. No *balungan* instruments are used, and the *pathetan* is completely free from the metrical constraints of a *balungan*: in this music lies perhaps the very essence of *pathet*.

A point to bear in mind in *pathet* analyses of larger compositions is the likelihood of ambivalence: most pieces show characteristics of more than one *pathet*, and it is even possible to speak of '*pathet* modulation'. A piece has its basic *pathet*, but often includes many phrases that lie outside it. This is analogous to a piece in a certain key which may touch on other keys, or actually establish them, before returning to the home key (which is the only one named in the title). The *balungan* tends to be treated by Westerners as an easy way into gamelan music theory, because some characteristics of *pathet* are gleaned from preliminary studies of its typical configurations. This is acceptable as long as it is remembered that it can only be a preliminary and incomplete analysis; however many *balungan* motifs are extracted from pieces, and even put into computers, they will never give the full picture of *pathet* as the Javanese perceive it (which must involve a consideration of every element of the piece, not just its *balungan*). Having said this, let us examine patterns which may be considered typical of particular *pathet*s. In keeping with Javanese priorities, *laras slendro* will be considered first:

What can be learned from this limited information? To begin with, the dots are significant in showing a gradual rise in tessitura through these three *pathet*s, and also in arriving at an idea of a note hierarchy. They will not have any bearing on how the patterns are played on the (one-octave) *balungan* instruments, but they are crucial to instruments (and the voice) that can reproduce them correctly. This general rise in tessitura is important in the all-night *wayang kulit* performance, which is traditionally accompanied by music in *laras slendro*, and is in three main sections. As the play travels through the life-cycle, from youth and inexperience, to the establishment of the individual in society, and finally to the wisdom of old age, when the trials and tribulations are finally resolved, so the music 'rises' through the *pathet*s: first *pathet nem*, then *pathet sanga*, and finally *pathet manyura*. To try and divorce *pathet* from human experience and consider it only in terms of sound patterns is therefore to miss an important point close to the Javanese. In other words, it is better translated as 'mood' rather than 'mode'. There are interesting parallels with Indian music, where this remark applies equally well. Perhaps the most important thing about an Indian *raga* is that it is an expression of feeling which flows from the heart of the musician to the hearts of the audience, instilling the bliss known as *rasa*. The Javanese have inherited this word and appreciate its importance, even if the precise context has changed over hundreds of years and miles.

If we examine the four-note patterns above a little further, some indicators of a hierarchy emerge. In each case one note of the *slendro* five is omitted, and this is regarded as the weakest in each *pathet*. The strongest in the group is the fourth; it often occurs at the end of phrases, when it may be further marked by a stroke on one of the punctuating gongs at the rear of the gamelan. The other three notes cannot easily be placed in a hierarchy, since their importance will vary according to context. It would not be wrong to suggest the following: in *slendro pathet nem*, the strongest note tends to be 2 and the weakest tends to be 1; in *slendro pathet sanga*, the strongest note tends to be 5 and the weakest 3; in *slendro pathet manyura*, the strongest note tends to be 6 and the weakest 5.

As stated earlier, in *pelog*, a difference of *pathet* often involves a difference of scale. The problem is that, instead of creating three different scales for each of the *pathet*s, there are really only two, distinguished primarily by the use of either note 1 (*bem*) or note 7 (*barang*), and accordingly named after the note in question. Note 4 is very much the odd one out. It is avoided altogether in the numbering of the *slendro* notes and is unavailable on some of the *pelog* instruments (for example, the *genders* and *gambang*) which will therefore either have the *bem* scale: 1 2 3 5 6 or the *barang* scale: 2 3 5 6 7. The latter is the typical material of *pathet barang*, while the former is the basis of *pathet lima* and *pathet nem*. Note 4 may be added to either, but it tends to be used sparingly, if at all, in *pathet barang*, and much more in *pathet nem* and *pathet lima*. The result is that many pieces become hexatonic and quite a few fully heptatonic, though it is unlikely that the underlying hierarchy will be disturbed, because the introduction of note 1 in *pathet barang* or note 7 in the other *pathet*s will be done with care and restraint. For example, the very long *Gendhing Babar Layar*, which is in *pelog pathet lima*, has a *balungan* totalling 640 beats based on the six notes from 1 to 6, and the note 7 is used just once!

As a general guide to the kinds of hierarchies which might be expected in the *pelog pathet*s, notes 1 and 5 will tend to be relatively strong in *pathet lima*; 3, 6, 2 and 5 in *pathet nem*; and 6 and 2 in *pathet barang* (which should not be confused with *pathet nem*, owing to the different scale). In *pelog* the real problem lies in distinguishing *pathet lima* from *pathet nem*, and even the Javanese sometimes have problems. One simple clue, if it can be heard, is that the open strings of the *rebab* are always tuned to 6 and 2 below, except in *pelog pathet lima* when they are lowered a step to 5 and 1.

If this introduction to *pathet* tends towards over-simplification, a more detailed examination would inevitably develop into a long and complicated account and is not feasible in the present context. Moreover the glimpse of what *pathet* seems to be about that is offered above would be obscured in the quest to establish what it actually is.

3 *Balungan*

Balungan literally means bones or skeleton, an apt name for what is often called the nuclear melody of a gamelan piece. It serves as a central melodic thread from which the parts of all the instruments of the gamelan can be determined, and experienced musicians will know how to relate their parts to the information of the *balungan*. For this reason, it is all that needs to be preserved, and collections of gamelan pieces in notation usually give just the *balungan*, plus a few indications of its form and punctuation (discussed below under *bentuk*). The *balungan* can flow in even notes (*balungan mlaku*), or by alternating notes and 'rests' which in practice will usually be the prolongation of the previous note, (*balungan nibani*), or by subdivided beats or combinations of notes and rests (*balungan ngadhal*). In all cases the notation will arrange the *balungan* into groups based on units of four beats (each beat is called a *keteg*) with a space between each group. The name for such a group is *gatra*, and this is a major organizational feature of *karawitan*. A *gatra* could be constructed in various ways, as noted, but the important point is always that the fourth beat is the most important, followed by the second. To call any the strong beat might be misleading, because there is no need for accentuation. The fourth beat of a *gatra* is a kind of centre of gravity or point of resolution, and musicians realizing other parts from the *balungan* will tend to focus on this last note of the *gatra*, steering their parts to coincide with it. If the fourth beat is a rest, it will usually be treated as a continuation of the previous note.

As an example of this, (showing mixtures of notes and rests, or the previous note prolonged), and also of subdivided beats (hence elements of *balungan mlaku* and *balungan ngadhal*, but not of *balungan nibani* which has a regular alternation of note and rest), here are the first eight *gatra*s of the piece called *Gendhing Babar Layar* (in *pelog*), with the important fourth note in each *gatra* indicated by an arrow:

The arrows suggest divisions into bars (eight bars of common time) but the essential difference is that the important beat is the fourth, rather than the first. In either case this beat is not necessarily stressed, and anyway it should be said that the problem is notational rather than aural. The reason for mentioning it is that Westerners usually learn *karawitan* through notation, and can easily be confused at first.

Because of its central importance, the *balungan* must be learned by everyone in the ensemble. Generally a beginner will be assigned to one of the group of instruments which play the *balungan*. One feature these instruments have in common is their restriction to an effective range of one octave. The paradox is that this restriction actually prevents them from playing the *balungan* as it really is. The true *balungan* (known in full as the *balunganing gendhing*, meaning 'the skeleton of the composition') usually spans a range of more than one octave, so what these instruments must do is rearrange it, with octave displacements, to fit it into their range. This is all right as long as one remembers that this is neither how the *balungan* would be sung nor how it would be notated. There is, for example, a crucial difference between a passage such as:

(a)

(i.e. a straight sequence of four descending notes), and the way the *balungan* instruments would play it:

(b)

(i.e. with a big leap upwards from the 1 to the 6). Those instruments which decorate the *balungan* with patterns ranging over more than one octave must follow the *balunganing gendhing*, and not this distorted version.

The whole concept of *lagu* (melody) in *karawitan* is fascinatingly elusive. If the *balunganing gendhing* is not played as it is conceived, where is it? The answer is: in the minds of the musicians. But even that is not the end of the story. The Javanese master, Sumarsam, argues the existence of what he calls the 'inner melody', which is not played by any single instrument but is a kind of intuitive melodic core which influences the movement and direction of the whole ensemble more than any single strand, including the *balunganing gendhing* itself. 'Inner melody is the melody that is sung by musicians in their hearts. Inner melody is the essence of melody in Javanese gamelan.'[3] Time and again one finds this emphasis on intuition and the heart before the head, as well as a reminder that this instrumental music has a vocal basis. It also seems typically Javanese to propose this elusive hypothesis of a melody that directs all others, and yet which is not performed and is not heard; nevertheless, this unheard force can serve as a vital analytical tool, helping to explain melodic motions in the ensemble which can sometimes appear to be at variance with the *balungan*. But of course its understanding and use are only granted to the expert musician in whose heart the inner melody is sung. It is hardly surprising that the inner melody is not notated. On the other hand the ease with which the *balungan* can be isolated and notated is a major reason for the importance given to it by theorists and musicians used to analysing and performing music through notation. Its value in the understanding, teaching, and preservation of gamelan music, especially among Westerners, cannot be denied, but it is best understood in its literal sense: a melodic skeleton.

4 *Irama*

Irama has often been confused with tempo, probably because the appropriate word, *laya* (still used today in India to denote tempo), is much less commonly employed. More accurately, *irama* is a concept of tempo relationships. While one may speak of one *irama* as being faster than another, such a distinction is only partially correct, because it may apply to some parts of the ensemble, whereas the reverse may apply to others. To look for a Western analogy: if the subject of a fugue is sounded in augmentation (i.e. twice as slow as normal), and yet the other parts move in shorter note values than they did against the original subject, the overall effect will not necessarily be one of a change of tempo. So it is in gamelan music: the *balungan* may sound at half its previous tempo while the other parts may sound at faster rates than before, yet this would not constitute a change of *laya* but instead one of *irama*.

Concentrating on the relationships between the parts of the ensemble, the Javanese have a very simple way of expressing *irama*. By taking one instrument (the *peking*) as reference, they compare its rate of activity with the *balungan*; thus, in one *irama*, the speed of the *balungan* may be fast and permit only one *peking* note per *balungan* note or beat, while in another it may be so slow that the *peking* may fit as many as sixteen notes per *balungan* note. These relationships are expressed in multiples of two, an important organizational principle of gamelan music, even though the pulses of different *irama*s do not necessarily have to be precisely twice as fast or slow. The main *irama*s are called *lancar* (fast, moving), *tanggung* (half, intermediate), *dados* or *dadi* (settled), *wiled* (which has the same connotation as *dados*; and significantly these are the main *irama*s for full-scale gamelan pieces), and *rangkep* (doubled). Each *irama*, expressed in terms of the relationship of *peking* to *balungan* is as follows:

irama lancar	one	
irama tanggung	two	
irama dados	four	} *peking* notes per one of *balungan*
irama wiled	eight	
irama rangkep	sixteen	

They are often given numbers as well, except for *irama lancar*. Thus, *irama tanggung* may be indicated as *irama* I, *irama dados* as *irama* II, *irama wiled* as *irama* III, and *irama rangkep* as *irama* IV. The pulse of *irama lancar* (that is, the *irama* where the *balungan* is moving at its fastest tempo) is not especially fast. A typical value would be around 120 *balungan* beats per minute. For this reason, a much faster *irama lancar* is sometimes played: a 'super *lancar*' called *irama gropak*; but the all-important relationships within it remain the same. Other relationships to the *balungan*, according to *irama*, apply to the other instruments of the gamelan, and some idea of how this happens will be given in Chapter 5.

The variations of tempo (*laya*) that can occur within any *irama* are grouped into three broad areas: *tamban* (slow), *sedheng* (medium), and *seseg* (fast). These may apply to whole sections where both *irama* and *laya* are stable, and also to the gradual change from one *irama* to another, which usually involves a change of tempo (for example, *irama tanggung* will slow down to go to *irama dados* and speed up to go to *irama lancar*).

5 *Bentuk* and *gendhing*

Bentuk means form (in Indonesian, suggesting a recent application to *karawitan*) which, in musical terms, means the organization of the *balungan* beyond the groupings of *gatras*, into larger sections and complete pieces. The generic term for a gamelan composition is *gendhing*, and this word is also used to preface the names of large-scale pieces with various formal organizations. Shorter forms have different names, for example: *lancaran, ketawang, ladrang, ayak-ayakan, srepegan,* and *sampak.*

Each of these *bentuk*s has characteristics which will apply to any piece of its kind: a type of melodic line and phrase-structure (discussed below in the section on *padhang-ulihan*), an underlying colotomic structure ('punctuating' pattern) on the various sets of gongs at the back of the gamelan, and very often a kind of mood and association. A *lancaran* is usually lively, while *srepegan*s and *sampak*s are used to accompany moments of instability (such as fights, entrances and exits) in *wayang,* and so on.

The main determinant of *bentuk* is the *gongan*: the melodic sentence between strokes of a large *gong.* This will often constitute an entire section, and in some cases an entire piece, and each *gongan* will be divided into a number of *kenongan*: phrases between strokes on the *kenong.* Many compositions in the *bentuk*s discussed below, especially *ketawang, ladrang* and the larger *gendhing,* have more than one section: in other words the *bentuk* structure (one *gongan*) is reduplicated throughout the whole piece (several *gongan*s). The *ladrang* form will be the focus of the next chapter, permitting a closer examination of one particular *bentuk.* In order to place it in the wider context of *bentuk,* some of the other main forms used in gamelan music will be briefly examined here, progressing from the shortest and simplest to some of the larger structures.

Lancaran

There are two types of *lancaran: balungan nibani,* in which there is a rest between each note of the *balungan,* and *balungan mlaku* where the *balungan* is a continuous series of notes. Either way there are sixteen *balungan* beats to the *gongan* (that is, between strokes on the *gong*). Because the tempo is relatively fast, the *gong* is usually the *gong suwukan,* the weightier *gong ageng* being reserved for the end of the *buka* (introduction), for the ends of main sections, and for the very end of the piece. (The two gongs do not play together.) The rest of the 'colotomic' section is shown with symbols commonly used in Java (see page xiv). Since the actual notes of the *balungan* vary from piece to piece they are not shown in the outline below; instead the symbol 0 is used to indicate the occurrence of *balungan* notes. (The *kempyang* is not played in *lancaran*s):

		×		×	∧	×	∨	×	∧	×	∨	×	∧	×	∨	×	∧
	nibani	.	0	.	0	.	0	.	0	.	0	.	0	.	0	.	(0)
Balungan																	
	mlaku	0	0	0	0	0	0	0	0	0	0	0	0	0	0	0	0 (0)

There is an apparent irregularity in this and subsequent *bentuk*s under examination owing to the deliberate omission of a *kempul* stroke in the space after the *gong*. (It must be remembered that the *gong* will already have sounded before the *bentuk* schemes shown in these notations begin: it will have been heard at the end of the *buka* introduction, and occurs again at the end of the cycle which may then be repeated.) This space is called *wela* (a Jogjanese term), and is an example of the Javanese sensitivity to orchestral density and balance. The more symmetrical form, involving four rather than three *kempul* strokes and filling the *wela*, would mean an undue thickening of the texture just after the large *gong* or *gong suwukan* has been struck and therefore while its powerful vibrations are still sounding.

Ketawang

This, too, has sixteen *balungan* beats per *gongan* (marked by the *gong ageng*; the *suwukan* is not used in this *bentuk*, or in the typical *ladrang* or larger *gendhings* discussed below) but the colotomic part is different from that of *lancaran*. The *kempyang* (shown by the symbol o) is also played:

o	×	o		o	×	o	∧		o	×	o	∨		o	×	o	∧
0	0	0	0		0	0	0	0		0	0	0	0		0	0	0 (0)	

Ladrang

This is rather like a double *ketawang*:

o	×	o		o	×	o	∧		o	×	o	∨		o	×	o	∧
0	0	0	0		0	0	0	0		0	0	0	0		0	0	0	0
o	×	o	∨		o	×	o	∧		o	×	o	∨		o	×	o	∧
0	0	0	0		0	0	0	0		0	0	0	0		0	0	0 (0)	

This applies to *irama*s *tanggung* and *dados* (the most usual *irama*s for *ladrang*s). In *irama wiled* (and *rangkep*) the number of *balungan* beats is doubled.

A relationship does, however, exist with the *lancaran*, *ketawang*, and *ladrang* forms, since each *gongan* will usually comprise either two *kenongan*s (as in a *ketawang*) or four (as in a *lancaran* or *ladrang*).

Ayak-ayakan

This and the next two *bentuk*s (*srepegan* and *sampak*) are particularly associated with the theatrical uses of gamelan (*wayang* and dance). They do sometimes occur in concert music (*klenengan*) but usually connected to other pieces in a kind of suite, rather than in isolation. Because of their essentially dramatic nature, they are subject to alteration in performance, with transitions and endings liable to occur at almost any point (determined by the dramatic action) and there is no real standardization in matters of length and form. What is given here is a typical Solonese version for each type. As in *lancaran*, the relatively frequent occurrence of notes played on the larger hanging gongs (shown by brackets) necessitates the use of the *gong suwukan* as well as the *gong ageng*. When each is to be used is determined in the actual performance; as a rule the *suwukan* is used more, the larger *gong* being reserved for ends of sections, often when the *balungan* note is 6, and so on. The notation usually indicates the *gong* without specifying which one, and this policy is followed here. The *kempyang* is not played in any of the three *bentuk*. A basic *ayak-ayakan* structure could be as follows:

```
x  ^  x  ^    x  ^  x  ^    x  ^  x  ^    x  ^  x  ^
.  0  . (0)   . 0  . (0)    . 0  . (0)    . 0  . (0)
```

and:

```
x  x^x  x^  x  x^x  x^  x  x^x  x^  x  x^x  x^
0 0 0 (0)  0 0 0 (0)  0 0 0 (0)  0 0 0 (0)
```

This is the scheme for *slendro pathet manyura*. In *pathet*s *nem* and *sanga* the gong comes at the end of phrases and is replaced at the end of the other *gatra*s by a *kempul*.

Srepegan and *Sampak*

The colotomic structure becomes a little denser and the tempo usually faster in *srepegan* (shown above), and also in *sampak*. The typical *talu* (equivalent to overture in a *wayang*) moves from the rather slow and dignified *ayak-ayakan* to the livelier *srepegan* and finally to the *sampak* in a continuous sequence, although the three pieces can also be played separately. As the excitement increases, so the melodic material simplifies. The *ayak-ayakan* is fairly free, the *srepegan* moves mainly in pairs of adjacent notes (for example 2 1 2 1 3 2 3 2), while the *sampak* is characterized by complete *gatra*s of the same note (6 6 6 6 3 3 3 3 2 2 2 2 etc.), with an unusually dense colotomic structure in which notes on the *kempul* occur as frequently as *balungan* notes, while the *kenong* actually moves at a faster rate:

Larger *gendhings*

These cannot be grouped under a single colotomic structure since the number of *balungan* beats per *gongan* varies from piece to piece and sometimes from section to section within the same piece. In general they are larger than any of the forms so far discussed: each section will usually be divided into two or four *kenongans* (sub-section between strokes on the *kenong*) and strokes on the large *gong* are most likely to occur after either 64, or 128 or 256 beats. A basic *gendhing*, like many *ketawang*s and *ladrang*s, is in two sections, called *merong* and *inggah*, linked by a short section called *ompak* (or *umpak*).

The full title of the *gendhing* will usually include information on the part played by the *kethuk*, so what seems a lowly and insignificant instrument is in fact a prime determinant of form. An example of such a complete title is: *Gendhing Tukung kethuk 4 kerep minggah 8 laras pelog pathet barang.* In this long title only the word *Tukung* refers to this particular piece. *Gendhing* means it is a (large-scale) gamelan composition, and the words at the end of the title carry the information on tuning and *pathet*. *Kethuk 4 kerep* means that there are four closely spaced (*kerep*) *kethuk* strokes per *kenong* stroke. The first of these *kethuk* strokes must fall at the end of the first *gatra* after the *gong*, and thence at the end of every other *gatra*. To show this, here is the first *kenongan* (section between strokes of the *kenong*, each one comprising 32 beats) of *Tukung*:

(a)

This pattern will continue throughout the *merong* (and the *ompak*, to the *inggah*). In *Tukung* the *merong* has four *kenongan*s, making a total of 128 beats between strokes on the *gong ageng* (thus four times as long as the *ladrang* form). The phrase '*minggah 8*' in the complete title of *Tukung* literally means 'rise (to) 8', still referring to the *kethuk* beats, but as they occur in the *inggah*. Thus, in this section there will be eight *kethuk* beats per *kenongan*. The first *kenongan* of the *inggah* of *Tukung* is:

(b)

Notice that the *kempyang* is also played in the *inggah*, but not in the *merong*. The *kethuk–kempyang* pattern in the *inggah* is the standard one, which is also used in the *ketawang* and *ladrang* forms. The *kempul*s (and also the *gong suwukan*) are not played in such *merong–inggah* forms. How often the sections are repeated and which tempi are used depends on the drummer. Thus such a piece could last anything from seven or eight minutes to half an hour or more.

71

Instead of the world *kerep* in the title, it is common to find *awis* or *arang* (literally 'rare'), both meaning the opposite of *kerep*, (in other words widely – rather than closely – spaced). If the *kethuk* strokes are *awis* (*arang*) the first one will fall at the end of the second *gatra* after the *gong*, and thereafter at the end of every fourth *gatra*. This will obviously make the *kenongan* (and indeed, the whole structure) longer than in the *kerep* type of *gendhing*. For example, the *merong* of *Gendhing Wedikengser* is *kethuk 4 awis* (as opposed to the *kethuk 4 kerep* of *Tukung*), and the first *kenongan* is as follows:

So each *kenongan* is twice the length of one in *Tukung*, making the *gongan* (four *kenongan*s) also twice as long, a total of 256 beats.

The different kinds of *gendhing* according to this *kethuk* classification may be summarized in the following table:

   i *kethuk 2 kerep minggah* 4
  ii *kethuk 4 kerep minggah* 4
 iii *kethuk 4 kerep minggah* 8
 iv *kethuk 8 kerep minggah* 16
   v *kethuk 2 awis minggah* 4
 vi *kethuk 2 awis minggah* 8
 vii *kethuk 4 awis minggah* 4
viii *kethuk 4 awis minggah* 8

The table indicates an obvious doubling (or quadrupling in one case) of the number of *kethuk* strokes from the *melong* to the *inggah*, with two exceptions, but in all cases the frequency of *kethuk* strokes is greater in the *inggah* where there is one per gatra. A *ladrang* is substituted for an *inggah* in the form called *ketawang gendhing* (or *gendhing ketawang*), in which the *merong* is *kethuk 2 kerep* but there are two *kenongan* (each consisting of four *gatras*) to the *gongan*. This substitution can also occur in other forms, in which case the title would become '*minggah ladrang*' (instead of the number of *kethuk* strokes); and many large *gendhing*s are extended by adding *ladrang*s or *ketawang*s after the *inggah*, or by connecting different compositions in a kind of suite, equivalent in length to a nineteenth-century symphony. Such large-scale forms will invariably be for the full gamelan, including vocal parts (especially the *sindhen*, for solo female singer). The main *gendhing* is usually classified as a *gendhing rebab* because the *rebab* is the leading melodic instrument. The *inggah* will probably have *ciblon* drumming and pass into *irama wiled*. This kind of music represents gamelan music at its most intricate. *Gendhing*s like *Tukung* and *Wedikengser*, on the other hand, belong to the smaller repertoire of *gendhing bonang*. Here, the *bonang*s are the principal 'embellishing' instruments. None of the softer instruments (*rebab*, *gender*, *gambang* etc.) nor the voice is included, and the drumming is restrained and often just on the *kendhang gendhing*. This gives such compositions a sparser sonority, with a more prominent *balungan* and generally louder dynamic than in *gendhing rebab*. They are often used at important events such as birth celebrations, weddings and sometimes circumcisions, and also at the commencement of palace ceremonies.

6 *Padhang-ulihan*

Karawitan is an art of balance. Just as in Western music tonality, form and phrase-structure are interconnected, so in *karawitan* are *pathet*, *bentuk* and *padhang-ulihan*. These last two words refer to the art of melodic phrasing, and *padhang-ulihan* are terms for balanced phrase-structures, adequately translated by 'antecedent' and 'consequent'. A *balungan* is therefore organized so that its *padhang-ulihan* structure follows the constraints of the *pathet* and in turn influences the *bentuk*.

Martopangrawit provides a clear definition, with a rather amusing extra-musical analogy, affording an insight into Javanese ways of thinking about music and human behaviour, which merits extensive quotation:

73

Padhang-ulihan is found in many disciplines – dance, carving, discourse, behavior, etc. In short, everything has padhang-ulihan. 'Padhang' ['bright', 'light', 'clear'] is something that is clear, but whose ultimate purpose is still unknown. That which clarifies the final purpose is 'ulihan' ['return', 'coming home']. For an example, let us imagine that we see a man walking to the bath, and we are unaware of his intentions. Will he take a bath, or wash his face, or merely inspect the condition of the bathwater? In other words, we know the padhang, but not the ulihan.

It is clear that each padhang may have 1,001 different ulihan. But it is necessary that there be a harmonious match between padhang and ulihan. If we saw a man enter the bath and straightaway lie down to take a nap, we would certainly laugh, since his intentions are not in agreement with the original appearance of his actions.

It is necessary to keep in mind that there are different levels of padhang-ulihan. For example, if a man goes to the bath with the intention of washing his face, this set of padhang-ulihan [i.e. action, final intention] can itself become a padhang [which will then be balanced by a larger ulihan].[4]

A simple example of *padhang-ulihan* analysis should clarify its principles. Taking one *gongan* of a very simple well-known *lancaran*, called *Ricik-ricik*:

The middle two *gatra*s are identical, and very similar to the first (since the last note is 5 in all three cases), while the fourth is different and gives a cadential feel, the 'answer' to the 'question', or the *ulihan* (U) to three *padhang*s (P), or even to just one if they are lumped together. (The process can be extended by considering the whole passage as a *padhang* or *ulihan* to another large section, not shown here.) This practice of joining small units into larger ones means that *padhang-ulihan* structures are embedded in larger ones (like Russian dolls) and in extended pieces this can lead to far more elusive structures, requiring more complex analysis. Such investigations are beyond the scope of this introduction, but it will be helpful to examine one more *bentuk*, in *ladrang* form, notably *Ladrang Wilujeng*, since this piece will become the basis of a detailed analysis in Chapter 5. There are two sections (*gongan*) and the structure is the same for each, so only one *gongan* need be given here. I choose the second (the *lik* section) because it is the part used in the detailed score at the end of Chapter 5:

This operates on three levels: *(a)* each even-numbered *gatra* acts as an *ulihan* to the preceding *padhang gatra*; *(b)* the first three pairs of *gatra*s each function as a *padhang* to the *ulihan* of the fourth pair; *(c)* the same three pairs, each one a *padhang*, can be combined into one large *padhang* (of six *gatra*s) to the same *ulihan* constituted by the fourth pair. (This is very similiar to the analysis of *Lancaran Ricik-ricik* above.) The colotomic structure of a piece therefore not only marks the form (*bentuk*) in terms of beats (a *kenong* stroke every so many beats, the *gong* after so many beats, etc.) but also reinforces the cadential feel of the *padhang-ulihan* structure. Without an understanding of this, and of the related issue of *pathet*, one may compose a *balungan* with 32 notes, a *gong* stroke at the end, plus all the other punctuations of a *ladrang*, and yet this will not guarantee that it is a genuine *ladrang*. This has caused problems for some non-Javanese composers who wish to borrow *bentuk* terms but whose compositions wander away from the *padhang-ulihan* and *pathet* constraints of the particular *bentuk*, preserving only its colotomic structure. To employ the terms correctly, therefore, brings us back to the first point of this section: an awareness of how the different elements of *karawitan* are inextricably linked.

7 Garap

To understand this word is to grasp how Javanese musicians approach *karawitan* and ensure its continuing vitality and creativity. Because the word 'improvisation' has no absolute meaning it must always be used with care and myriad qualifications. To state that gamelan music is improvised is likely to convey the impression of a freedom, even looseness, which it does not have; but to try and close the matter there would do the greater disservice of denying it that element of choice and interpretative spontaneity that is crucial to any great musical tradition. *Garap*, meaning 'treatment' (literally 'working on'), refers to the way a musician realizes another part from a given one (the *balungan*, or, more accurately, the elusive 'inner melody'). A similar situation would arise in our culture when one is harmonizing a given melody at the keyboard or realizing a figured bass. In each case the act involves improvisation, but a context is established and a framework within which the realization will be acceptable but beyond which it will probably be judged unclear, inappropriate, and even wrong. No problem is thought to have but one solution, and *garap* is the art of finding the solution that fits best but does not necessarily preclude others – nor, indeed, the desirability of variations. A *gender* player, for example, may study a given *balungan* and choose patterns from the repertoire to suit it according to its shape, direction and *pathet*, but may play any one pattern in a variety of ways. *Garap* therefore also involves an act of musical analysis in performance. The better the musician, the more varied the repertoire and performance and the more sure-footed the *garap*. The only likely *impasse* is if the given material (*balungan*) itself obscures any of the finely balanced principles of *karawitan* which govern and focus the *garap*. The whole of the next chapter is a study of *garap* in its broad sense of performance practice. It investigates how gamelan players might approach a given piece and decide what each instrument will play, according to its idiomatic repertoire and the guiding principles of *karawitan*. This *garap* may then represent only the solution on that particular occasion. The same musicians could vary it slightly on other occasions, and another group of musicians might find a substantially different *garap* as their basis. The flexibility and impermanence (which are not quite synonymous with improvisation) of *garap* make the idea of a 'score' (such as the one at the end of the next chapter) of a gamelan piece contrary to Javanese musical thought – almost a contradiction in terms – and it can only be offered as a study guide, without any Western implication of a fixed, definitive version.

Notes

1 Tables, comparing a wide range of gamelans and their tunings (expressed in Hertz numbers and Cents), are given in Kunst, op. cit., pp. 572–5.
2 In Judith Becker and Alan H. Feinstein, eds., *Karawitan*, Vol. I (1984), pp. 45, 47.
3 Ibid., p. 262.
4 Ibid., p. 66.

Chapter 5

Theory into practice:
gamelan music in performance

Having considered the structure and manufacture of the instruments of the Javanese gamelan and laid the theoretical foundations of the music, we now turn to the musical function of each instrument within the total group. As a rule, the largest instruments are placed to the rear and the smallest to the front. This also means that the louder and deeper-pitched instruments, which play slow-moving parts, are to the rear, while the softer and higher-pitched instruments, playing faster music, are to the fore. The point to be stressed in this deliberate generalization and simplification is that a clear visual and aural logic may be discerned in the beauty of the gamelan, both by the eye and the ear. This chapter aims, by avoiding complexity as much as possible, to bring out the wonderful logic and simplicity of the principles that govern the music.

The process by which this will be achieved is inevitably one of dissection and stripping down; and it is important to stress at the outset, as Kunst has done, that gamelan music must first be heard and appreciated as an aural whole:

> It is undeniable that the primarily important thing is precisely this experience of the orchestral sound heard as one single, pure entirety; intellectual analysis should come later, at any rate for those who like to make themselves, as far as possible, conscious of the phenomena coming under their notice, so that intuitive apprehension and intellectual probing may supplement each other, and, together, provide an enjoyment of a higher order than either function could provide unaided.[1]

Of course, the only way to experience the sound as a single, pure entirety is to hear it, preferably live or else on a recording of the best quality. But the intellectual analysis of the parts that go to make up this entirety (even though the whole is so much more than the sum of its parts) can be attempted in writing, and this is the stage we have now reached.

It is a tradition among musicologists to divide the gamelan into three main groups. Although one of these groups is a rather random mixture of some of the most important and beautiful instruments, the classification works well enough, especially for the other two groups, the first two in the following discussion.

1 *Balungan*

We may start with the central group, both in the sense of physical location within the gamelan and in terms of pitch register, medium pulse, and centrality of importance to the whole composition. This group plays the melodic outline on which the entire musical structure is based. The *balungan* is a prime determinant of the other parts, thus it is unnecessary to include them in notations of gamelan compositions, the assumption being that, once it has been learned, the part for any instrument can be derived from it.

The instruments which play the *balungan* are of the *wilah* variety. It is important to emphasize that instrumental functions within the Javanese gamelan tend to be fixed; thus it is much easier to explain the structures and functions within a gamelan than, for example, the Western symphony orchestra, where there is no longer any clear one-to-one relationship between instrument and function (for example, the violins do not always play the melody, or the violas the accompaniment, or the cellos the bass line). The *balungan* instruments in the gamelan can therefore be regarded as unchangingly *balungan* instruments. They are the *saron barung* (usually known simply as *saron*), the *saron demung* (usually known simply as *demung*), the *saron panerus* (usually known by its nickname of *peking*) and the *slenthem*. The typical gamelan will have two *saron barung* (both in *slendro* and *pelog*) and one each of the other instruments (also in both tunings). These five *balungan* instruments span a range of four octaves, from the lowest note of the *slenthem* to the highest note of the *peking*. The 'unison' *balungan* (there are important deviations, which are examined below) is therefore widely distributed across the compass of the gamelan, yet at the same time embedded in the centre of the group and the composition, and, despite its crucial importance, usually not aurally dominant. It is the policy of this book to explain a small amount of music in some detail, rather than to attempt to cover a wide repertoire. The important (and convenient) point is that the principles operating in one single piece may be applied extensively to virtually all the classical repertoire. For this reason, one piece will be examined to the extent that it will be possible to combine the functions of the main instruments in the gamelan into a kind of 'score' of the composition. This is the very well-known *Ladrang Wilujeng*, which has the added advantage of being performed in both *slendro* and *pelog* (a possibility which applies to a sizeable minority of gamelan pieces). The piece has the typical two-section form, usually performed A–A–B, and repeated *ad libitum*. The second section is called the *lik* (or *ngelik*), and the first section is sometimes (though not universally) called the *ompak* (not to be confused with the transition passage of the same name in larger *gendhings*). The notation of the *balungan*, as it would be found in a book of gamelan music, is as follows:

In *slendro* (*pathet manyura*):
First part – :

Second part – (*lik*):

In *pelog* (*pathet barang*):

(*lik*):

This *balungan*, fitted into one octave, is played by the *saron*s, *demung* and *slenthem*. A variation, known as *pinjalan*, may be employed by the *demung*, *slenthem* and *saron*s, and this will be discussed below. The *peking*, on the other hand, must always play a variation of the *balungan* except in the fastest *irama*s (*lancar* and *gropak*). Since this *ladrang* (and most others) is basically in *irama tanggung* and *irama dados*, the *peking* part is more complex than the given *balungan*. *Ladrang Wilujeng* will start in *irama tanggung* and either continue for one or more complete statements in this *irama*, or slow down very soon (by the end of the second line) to *irama dados*. The *peking* will therefore begin by playing two notes to one of *balungan*, changing to four when the *irama* has stabilized in *irama dados*. In the faster *irama* it is usual simply to double the *balungan* note, and it would not be incorrect to play it four times in *irama dados*. A better version, and far more interesting one, however, is a simple variation known as *selang-seling* (meaning alternate). Once the principles are grasped it is easy to play the *selang-seling* part instantly against any *balungan*. Each pair of notes of the *balungan* is taken; the first may be regarded as weak and the second strong. Each note is played twice in such a way that the strong note coincides in the *balungan* and *peking* part, while the *peking* also strikes the strong note against the weak note in the *balungan*. This can be shown quite simply in notation, taking the first *gatra* of *Wilujeng*:

This is divided into two pairs:

and the *peking* realization (*selang-seling*, in *irama dados*) is as follows:

Two eventualities remain to be considered: the occurrence of repeated notes and of rests. In effect they are one and the same since the *peking* treats rests as a continuation of the preceding *balungan* note, and the important rule is that the *peking* continues to play even when the other *balungan* instruments rest. What does not happen, however, in *selang-seling* is the straight repetition of repeated notes in the *balungan*, for example (in *Wilujeng*):

Instead, an auxiliary note, adjacent to the actual *balungan* note, must be inserted as a weak note, so that the characteristic line of the *selang-seling* variation can be maintained. The choice of auxiliary note will of course be between two (except when the *balungan* note falls at either extreme of the instrument), and the *peking* player must make the choice according to the line of the *balungan*, its *pathet*, and the general feel of the piece. Sometimes even both auxiliaries can be used. In the case of *Wilujeng* just given, 2 would be a better, and more obvious, choice than 5 (but both could be incorporated into the line), so the part could be:

(remembering that the *peking* plays as though the note 3 of the *balungan* is repeated in the rests).

While the remaining *balungan* instruments (usually a couple of *sarons*, one *demung* and one *slenthem*) normally play the *balungan* in its basic form, a variation – mentioned earlier – called *pinjalan* (which means the hopping of a flea!) is often used in *irama dados* on the *demung*, *slenthem* and *sarons*, though usually confined to the *pelog* tuning. In this case (assuming that the *peking* is playing *selang-seling*) the 'straight' *balungan* is not played by any instrument, and this can pose problems of audibility for the inexperienced player or listener! Taking first the *demung* part of *pinjalan*, a clear connection with the *selang-seling* variation of the *peking* emerges. In effect, the *demung* plays the *selang-seling* part in single rather than double notes, while the *slenthem* plays the other note of the *peking* part, giving a kind of off-beat throb:

(It is because the *slenthem* is generally the most important and audible *balungan* instrument that this persistent off-beat pattern can confuse the beginner.) As with *selang-seling*, rests and repeated notes present slight problems. It could be argued that a strict imitation of the *selang-seling* line would be possible, but in fact a more interesting line is used. Below are the 'solutions' to the rests and repeated notes of the *pelog* version of *Wilujeng*:

83

The departures from the basic *selang-seling* pattern are thus confined to the second halves of a) and b).

In *pinjalan* the *saron*s (*barung*) keep in rhythmic unison with the *balungan*, but play only the notes that occur on the strong second and fourth beats of each *gatra*, for example:

In certain circumstances, usually in *wayang* music, the *saron*s between them play the *pinjalan* pattern of the *demung* and *slenthem* (while those instruments play the straight *balungan*) and this re-instrumentation is known as *kinthilan*.

The score of the *lik* of *Wilujeng* at the end of this chapter is in the *slendro* tuning, and the *saron*s, *demung*, and *slenthem* play the straight *balungan*.

2 Colotomic Structure

The *balungan* is central in terms of structure, instrumental layout and also *irama*. To the rear of the gamelan are the larger gongs which play at the slowest rate, in keeping with the aural and visual logic discussed earlier. They collectively perform what the musicologists call the 'colotomic function': in other words, they punctuate the *balungan*. How they do this depends on the *bentuk* of the piece. *Wilujeng* is an example of *bentuk ladrang*. This means that there are 32 *balungan* beats between strokes on the *gong ageng*. This instrument has the lowest pitch in the gamelan and plays the least often, yet its importance is in relation to its size. It is very easy to play, as are all the colotomic instruments, yet the *gong* player must be very secure in the knowledge of the *balungan*, since a missed stroke or one in the wrong place is probably the most destructive gesture in gamelan music. For this reason the *gong* player is often a veteran musician, respected, like the instrument, above all others. In notation the *gong* stroke is shown by brackets around the *balungan* note it accompanies.

Usually in the same rack as this *gong* are the smaller hanging gongs (*kempul*), and also the *gong suwukan*, which is not normally used in *ladrangs*. The *kempul* is played at the end of the third, fifth and seventh *gatra*s of the eight-*gatra ladrang* form. The omission (*wela*) of a *kempul* stroke at the end of the first *gatra* is, as we have already noted, one of the refinements of gamelan music (see p. 68).

The choice of *kempul* note is determined by the *balungan* and the *pathet*. Since a typical gamelan will have no *kempul* for note 2 and sometimes note 3, as a very general rule (which applies to *Wilujeng*) *kempul* 6 can be used for either of those notes, while any other *balungan* note can be found among the *kempul*. On the rare occasions that *pelog* 4 must be used on either the *kempul* or *kenong*, the near unison *slendro* 5 in the typical *tumbuk nem* gamelan (in which note 6 coincides in *slendro* and *pelog*) may be borrowed.

The *kenong* plays at the end of even-numbered *gatras*. This means that a *kenong* stroke accompanies the large *gong*. In slow music it is often the practice to delay both the *kenong* and *gong* strokes until slightly after the beat. In the case of the *kenong* this enhances its audibility since it is otherwise easily masked. In the *ladrang* form, the *kenong* beats come at the end of the second, fourth, sixth and eighth *gatras*. All notes are available in the *kenong* section of the typical gamelan, but the *kenong* note does not necessarily always coincide with the *balungan* note. In *Wilujeng* the second *gatra* ends on note 6, but, as is so typical of gamelan music, the *kenong* has an anticipatory function to the extent that, should a repeated note come immediately after a *kenong* beat, then the *kenong* must play that note rather than the actual *balungan* note with which it coincides. Thus, at the end of the second *gatra* the *kenong* note will be 3, not 6. The same rule applies in the *lik* at the end of the fourth *gatra*, where the *kenong* note will be 6 rather than 2, and at the end of the sixth *gatra*, where it will be 1 (*slendro*) or 7 (*pelog*) rather than 6. This practice is given the apt name of *plesedan*, meaning 'sliding' or 'slipping'.

The *kethuk* and *kempyang* present no problem with regard to notes, since there is only one *kethuk* and one *kempyang* for *slendro*, and likewise for *pelog*. Although there are two gongs in each set, and each has a name, the two effectively constitute one instrument, which is always played by the same player using one mallet. The *kempyang* is always played with the *kethuk*, but the *kethuk* may be used on its own in certain kinds of pieces. The typical pattern which generally applies whenever both are used, as in the case in the *ladrang* form, is for the *kethuk* stroke to fall on the relatively strong second beat of each *gatra*, sandwiched between two strokes on the *kempyang* (on the weaker first and third beats). The strongest fourth beat is taken by the stronger *kenong*, *kempul* and *gong*, so that the whole colotomic section interlocks in a balanced manner. While the *kempyang* is always played with a single open stroke, in all but the fastest music the *kethuk* is struck with two or more strokes, played in rapid succession and damped. (Notations, however, always indicate a single stroke. Many notations in fact do not bother to indicate the *kethuk* and *kempyang* parts at all, since they are known for any particular *bentuk*.)

3 Embellishment

This word is often used, for want of a better, to classify the various instruments placed at the front of the gamelan which play at a faster rate than the *balungan*. Again, what is played must relate to the *balungan*, and each instrument paraphrases it in some way from a repertoire of idiomatic sequences chosen by the player to fit the *balungan*. Collectively these many instruments (to which must be added the voice) weave intricate polyphony around the *balungan*, putting not only the flesh and skin on to the skeleton, as it were, but also the finest clothes and most precious jewels. Gamelan music is inconceivable without at least some of these instruments, and the more refined the composition the more will be used. (An important exception is the repertoire of *gendhing bonang*, which are relatively stark.) The functions of the main embellishing instruments will be examined, one instrument at a time, but so elaborate is the repertoire of all these instruments that entire books are devoted to each one. The reader may expect here only the simple, basic versions, as could be played by a competent rather than expert ensemble, and should bear in mind that, as in any good music, there are exceptions to all the rules, and no amount of written descriptions and notations can ever capture all the refinements and subtleties of the music as it is actually performed. This, incidentally, is also where the question of improvisation comes in. To summarize a difficult and elusive topic, improvisation – such as it can be said to exist – lies essentially in the variation of the basic pattern, and the choice of that basic pattern (which is the subject of *garap*). Variation is more a matter of inflexion than complete transformation, and the listener would generally be able to discern the basic pattern (which is the concern of this study) through all the subtle changes that an individual player might impose.

Bonang barung and *bonang panerus*

The main embellishing instruments of the louder style (*soran*) of music, and arguably the easiest to play, are the two *bonang*s. Since the *bonang barung* is the more important the main reference will be to it. There are three main styles or *garap*: (i) *gembyang* (or *gembyangan*); (ii) *mipil* (or *pipilan*); (iii) *imbal* (or *imbalan*).

(i) *Gembyang*

This word means 'octave', and the essence of the pattern is the off-beat sounding of two notes an octave apart. It is used in *irama lancar* (and *gropak*), and therefore it is most appropriate to examine the pattern within compositions of the *lancaran* variety, rather than in a slower one such as *Wilujeng*. Here is part of the *balungan* of the *lancaran* quoted earlier on p. 74, entitled *Ricik-ricik*:

The *bonang* player will select the final note, called the *seleh* note, of each *gatra* (shown by arrows in this notation) as the basis for the *gembyang*, and then play this note in octaves on the first and third beats (in this case rests) of the relevant *gatra*. This means – and it is important to emphasize this point as typical of gamelan music – that the embellishment *anticipates* the *balungan*. This can best be seen in the notation below where the *gembyang* note changes from 5 to 6. The *bonang panerus*, typifying the logic of gamelan music, parallels its 2 : 1 pitch relationship to the *bonang barung* (since it is pitched an octave higher) with a version of the embellishment that is twice as fast. It would be more accurate to say that the *bonang panerus* gives the *illusion* of playing twice as fast in *gembyangan*, rather than literally doing so, since what it plays is a kind of syncopated pattern around the *bonang barung*, choosing the notes in exactly the same way:

Some *bonang panerus* players perform instead a triplet rhythm: , but the version given above is more common.

(ii) *Mipil*

Here, the *bonang* parts are essentially an oscillation between pairs of *balungan* notes, performed in *irama tanggung* and *dados*, and occasionally in *irama wiled*. In *irama tanggung* the *bonang* pattern is called *mipil lamba* and in the other *irama*s it is called *mipil rangkep*. (Occasionally *mipil lamba* may be played in *irama dados*, creating a majestic effect. This depends on the piece and the feeling that the *bonang* player wishes to convey.) Both *irama tanggung* and *dados* may be used in *Wilujeng*, so let us take the first *gatra* of the piece to examine these two kinds of *mipil*:

The *bonang* splits the *gatra* into two pairs of notes, making sure that the second note of each pair (the stronger beat) coincides with the *balungan*. In *mipil lamba* the *bonang* moves at twice the speed of the *balungan*, so each pair is played twice:

89

In performance, however, it is preferable to omit the bracketed note, leaving it to the *balungan* instruments. In *mipil rangkep*, the rate is four *bonang* notes per *balungan* beat, which would be:

But to perform it like this would be intolerably dull and would give the *bonang* undue prominence, so, as in *mipil lamba*, it is the practice to omit at least one note (which would be the fourth and twelfth notes in this example), and the most stylish way of playing *mipil rangkep* actually omits three per pair of *balungan* notes:

The *bonang panerus* will play the same as the *bonang barung*, but twice as fast, and again it is necessary to omit notes in order to give the line a more interesting shape and also to avoid thickening the texture, and even to reduce fatigue on the player's part! In *irama tanggung* the *bonang panerus* is already playing *mipil rangkep*, therefore it is not customary to talk about *mipil lamba* with reference to this instrument.

It is not always possible to follow the *balungan* automatically in this way. Certain patterns of notes demand special treatment, often because of a relatively wide leap, as in the last two notes of the very next *gatra* of *Wilujeng*:

where the *bonang*s play:

The next *gatra* of *Wilujeng* consists of a repeated note and two rests:

The simplest realization of this is the same note four times (3 3 3 3) which is what is discussed here, but it is worth pointing out, as an example of the flexibility of gamelan music, that a more sophisticated rendering would treat the two rests not as continuations of the note 3 but as note 6 (twice). This apparent anomaly is best explained by the concept of inner melody (discussed in Chapter 4), so, while the *balungan*

suggests a prolongation of the note 3 in the rests, the inner melody (led by the *rebab*) moves on to note 6. In any case, for this *gatra* involving a repeated note, *gembyang* must be used, rhythmically altered to fit the slower tempo. Treating the rests as prolongations of the note 3, in *irama dados* the *bonangs* play:

But a better version, giving a feeling of triple metre, is:

(In both *bonang* parts just the double notes could be played, the notes for left hand alone omitted.)

Another problem arises in pieces which employ *balungan nibani*, where a *balungan* note alternates with a rest, for example:

For any *irama* slower than *irama lancar* (and that includes the majority) the *gembyang* pattern, shown earlier for *Lancaran Ricik-ricik*, cannot be used. Neither can the regular *mipil* pattern, because each half *gatra* contains one note, rather than two. Effectively, the *bonang* adds a note in order to preserve the oscillating feel of *mipil*. Taking the *seleh* note (the final, crucial note of each *gatra*) the *bonang* begins the *gatra* by

playing the note above and the note below the *seleh* note, and ends with
the *seleh* note itself alternating with one of these notes, for example:

(iii) *Imbal*

This is characterized by the interlocking of an on-beat pattern on the
bonang barung with an off-beat pattern on the *bonang panerus*, thus
placing the latter instrument on a more equal footing with the former
than in the other styles. *Imbal* may be played in the same *irama*s as
mipil. It is also the main style in those slower than *irama dados*, and it
may also be used in the fastest *irama*s, especially in modern gamelan
compositions. The main determining factor as to whether *imbal* or *mipil*
should be used is the drum. As a general rule, *imbal* goes with the *ciblon*
drum while *mipil* goes with the *kendhang gendhing* (*kendhang I*) and
also the combination of *kendhang gendhing* and *ketipung* (*kendhang
II*). Thus, when the drummer changes to the *ciblon*, the *bonang*s tend to
switch to *imbal* after a short delay, usually at the *gong*.

The idea of *imbal* can be shown very simply by selecting first a pair of
notes on the *bonang barung*, with a gap of one note between them, (for
example, 1 and 3). The *bonang panerus* will then take a pair of notes,
similarly gapped, so that one of them fits between the two *bonang
barung* notes, (for example 2 and 5). Together, the two patterns may be
notated thus:

The *bonang panerus* plays in its lower octave so that the two parts interlock within the same octave, with the *bonang panerus* notes above those of the *bonang barung*. In the example above a resultant ostinato figure is created: 2 1 5 3 which moves twice as fast as either *bonang* part on its own. The maintenance of such an ostinato over what would be long stretches of time in the slower tempi could become monotonous, and this is avoided by breaking up the *imbal* line with a series of cadential patterns called *sekaran*. This word means 'flowering', and it is as if the *imbal* line is the stem that blossoms into flower at the end of each phrase. Usually the end of the phrase means the end of the *gatra*, unless there is a rest at this point, in which case it is usual for the *imbal* to continue. The *bonang* players will have a repertoire of *sekaran*s, each for a particular *seleh* note, and two of them will be given later.

Imbal (and *ciblon* drumming) are not used in *Wilujeng*, but some short and simple pieces (as well as larger, complex ones) allow all three styles of bonang embellishment. *Lancaran Tropongbang, laras pelog pathet nem* enables us to observe the three styles applied to a single extract of *balungan*. Being a relatively loud and vigorous piece, it is introduced by the *bonang (barung)*. Gamelan pieces begin with an introductory phrase, called *buka* (which means 'opening'), played on a solo instrument accompanied by the *kendhang*. In louder, faster pieces the *buka* is usually played on the *bonang barung*, and in softer, slower pieces it is usually played on the *rebab*, or perhaps the *gender*, or sometimes sung. The *buka* identifies the piece and also indicates tempo and the point where the full gamelan enters. To introduce *Lancaran Tropongbang*, the *bonang barung* plays the phrase:

After four notes, the *bonang* is joined by the *kendhang*, and on the last note comes a stroke on the large *gong*, also the *kenong*, and the *balungan* instruments enter, playing the note 5. The complete *balungan*, from this point, is as follows, with each line played twice:

It can be played in *irama*s *lancar*, *tanggung*, and *dados*. For present purposes, it is only necessary to give part of the piece (arbitrarily the first and last *gatra*s) as an example of how the *bonang* players may treat it. In *irama lancar* they play *gembyang*. Is this fastest tempo the *balungan* is often modified from *balungan mlaku* to *balungan nibani*, and both are indicated:

In *irama tanggung* they play *mipil lamba*:

95

In *irama dados* they play *mipil rangkep*:

Still in *irama dados*, the drum may change to *ciblon*, in which case the *bonang*s will play *imbal* and *sekaran*:

From these extracts it is as apparent to the eye as to the ear that *imbal* and *sekaran* represent the densest and liveliest of *bonang* patterns, paralleling *ciblon* among drumming styles. The liveliness of the *imbal* and *ciblon* combination is usually further enhanced by *keplok*, which is rhythmic clapping by the singers and anyone else with their hands free.

Rebab

With the various instruments of the softer kind among the embellishing group we come to the most refined, subtle and complex aspects of gamelan music. To do justice to these instruments (to which must be added the human voice) in even the same way as for the *bonang*s, offering a representative summary, would go far beyond the scope of this book.

Instead, we will return to *Ladrang Wilujeng* and examine a selection from the repertoire of these instruments appropriate to this composition and typical of gamelan music in general. The *rebab* part is among the most fluid; even when it relates closely to the *balungan* it is performed in a kind of rubato manner so that it never quite synchronizes with the *balungan*. The same applies to the *sindhen* (the part for solo female singer) and the *suling* (bamboo flute) melodies. They are, if anything, rhythmically freer than the *rebab* line and cannot really be accurately notated in the cipher notation. In the case of the *rebab*, however, many notations are available. These indicate a simple rhythm, clearly related to the *balungan*, and an absence of ornamentation. They are useful in understanding the basic idea of the *rebab* part, and can even be used in teaching. For this reason a simple *rebab* part will be given for *Wilujeng*, with the reminder that different players will perform it in different ways, employing rubato and ornaments such as turns, slides, accents and vibrato.

One point which should be made about the *rebab*, voice, and *suling* is that they are the only true *sustained* sounds in the gamelan. Those who may find them incongruous in the homogeneity of the bronze sonorities should bear this in mind. The *rebab*, more than any other member, exploits this potential to bind the sounds of the gamelan together and create a legato effect which is so aesthetically pleasing in this music. (For reasons explained in the notes on Notation, p. xiii–xvi, the notation indicates rests where in fact the *rebab* will almost certainly be sustaining the previous note.) The *suling* does the same thing, but only intermittently. Circular breathing (snatching breaths while still blowing, so that the sound is not broken) is practised in Indonesia (for example on the *suling gambuh* of Bali) but, for some reason, has not been applied to the gamelan under discussion.

The other obvious attribute of the voice, the *rebab* and the *suling* is that they are the only instruments of the ensemble which may vary their pitch, and actually produce notes outside the fixed *slendro* and *pelog* systems. The solo female voice and the *rebab* exploit this possibility in the tuning known as *barang miring*, to produce certain pitches between the notes of the *slendro* scale to great expressive effect. *Barang miring* is usually inserted into certain *slendro* pieces to express sadness or pathos, and another name for it, *minir*, is close to the European 'minor', with its similar associations of mood.

An additional point about the *rebab* is that it (rather than the *bonang*) usually pays the *buka* in *Wilujeng*. This is because this piece is performed in the softer style, giving the more subdued embellishing instruments, led by the *rebab*, an important role.

The word most often used to cover the multitude of patterns for these instruments, especially the *gender*, is *cengkok*. This means the line traced by a particular instrument from one point (of the *balungan*) to another. The main determining factor is the *seleh* note and a *cengkok* is usually of one *gatra*'s duration, from one *seleh* note to the next, although a substantial number of *cengkok*s last for two *gatra*s. The *cengkok*s discussed below are all conceived in terms of the structure and *irama* of *Wilujeng*. Parts for instruments like *rebab*, *gender* and *gambang* comprise series of *cengkok*s chosen to fit the particular *balungan*. To put the matter very simply, it is the ordering of the *cengkok*s rather than the *cengkok*s themselves which is peculiar to a given piece. (This is another reason why the study of one piece as typical of a whole repertoire is valid.)

Gender barung and gender panerus

As with the *bonang*s, the *barung* instrument is more important than the *panerus* and more attention must be given to it. Because the *gender* (*barung*) alone among all gamelan instruments has a part consisting of two continuous lines, its material is rich in harmonic as well as melodic

98

possibilities, encompassing the refinements and complexities of *pathet* and other aspects of gamelan music. This virtual self-sufficiency makes the *gender* satisfying to play as a solo instrument, and the musician who understands and can perform its vast repertoire of *cengkok*s, introducing innumerable subtle variations, is indeed a master of gamelan. In Java probably more time and space in publications are devoted to this instrument than any other. One way of teaching is to give some of the commonest *cengkok*s so that a large number of pieces can be played at a relatively early stage. To restrict ourselves to *Wilujeng* can give a useful sample, with the emphasis on simplicity and on the kind of material taught to beginners. It is customary to give every *gender cengkok* a name (more so than for other instruments), but the names are by no means standardized, nor even known to all players. In *Wilujeng* a *cengkok* which may be frequently used is generally called *kuthuk kuning gembyang* (literally 'yellow chick octave'; musicians often remember *cengkok*s from related vocal tunes and their texts). It fills one *gatra* ending on 6, where the previous *gatra* ended with rests after 6 or 2. In its simplest form (as it appears in *irama dados* in the score) it is notated:

This is later varied to:

To give an idea of how the element of improvisation may be introduced to vary the *cengkok*s, here are three more versions of this particular *cengkok*:

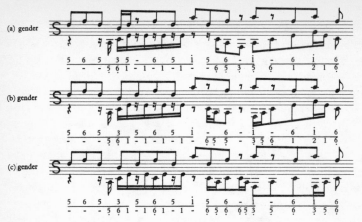

Notice how the right-hand part (upper line) is relatively unchanged, the focus of activity being on the left hand (lower line), which moves at a faster rate than the right hand. This is a characteristic feature of *gender* playing. The notation suggests that the half notes in the left hand are evenly spaced. In performance, however, it is very common to alter this to a dotted rhythm.

The *gender panerus*, pitched an octave above the *gender barung*, usually plays twice as fast. Its part is, however, less complicated than that of the *gender barung*, because the two hands do not normally play together, the rapidly moving line being distributed between them. It is possible to reduce the repertoire of this instrument to a set of phrases, applicable to *slendro* and *pelog*. There is a similarity between this repertoire and the *imbal-sekaran* repertoire of the *bonangs*, insofar as a basic phrase is repeated, ending with a *sekaran* to fit the *seleh* note. Confining the examples to *laras slendro pathet manyura* (which applies to *Wilujeng*) the ostinato phrase in *irama dados* is as follows:

This is repeated for the first three notes of the *gatra* and a *sekaran* is played on the fourth note, determined by that actual note. Some *sekarans* are shown in the provisional score of *Ladrang Wilujeng*, and it must be emphasized that this very basic repertoire, although perfectly acceptable, will be varied and added to by an experienced player.

Another convenient point about this simple repertoire is that it may also be played on the plucked instrument, the *siter*, and for this reason that instrument is not included in the score. In performance, it is more than likely that the *siter* will not play exactly the same as the *gender panerus*. For example, the ostinato pattern could be

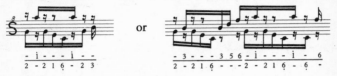

which are still quite close to the *gender panerus* version.

Gambang

This instrument combines the speed of the *gender panerus* with the continuous two-handed playing of the *gender barung*. Two factors, however, make the *gambang* easier to play than this latter instrument. One is that no damping technique is necessary, since the wooden bars have less resonance; and the other is that, for most of the time, the two hands play an octave apart, and not in the more independent and complex manner of the *gender barung*. *Gambang* notations do not therefore need to show the lines for each hand; just the left-hand part is given, with the assumption that the right hand will follow it an octave higher. As with everything else, a good player will produce more interesting *cengkok*s, involving some departure from this 'unison' style, with syncopation, rapidly repeated notes, and so on. For example, the *cengkok* segment shown in the score as

may be played:

or by omitting notes (possibly the third and fifth in the right hand), while the *cengkok* at the beginning of the *lik* may be performed with a more interesting rhythm (which – according to some Javanese – imitates a limping animal):

The notation in the score, however, represents one of many possibilities for the *gambang* which is both simple and adequate.

Suling

As the only wind instrument used in the gamelan, the *suling* adds a distinctive timbre. Its part is among the freest, and consequently, the hardest to notate. Apart from the human voice, the only other comparable instrument in the gamelan is the *rebab*. They are the only two instruments without fixed pitches, and both are played with a vocal fluidity. The crucial difference, however, is that the *rebab* is far more important and its part is both continuous and relatively easy to notate. The little phrases from the *suling* which occur intermittently are so free in rhythm as to be almost impossible to notate in the cipher system, while staff notation would give them unwarranted air of rhythmic complexity, and, far worse, fix them into that complexity. Few attempts appear to exist at notating the *suling* part. The normal method is to learn a few *cengkok* phrases which can then be shaped in performance according to aural experience, and the determinants of the *pathet*, melodic line and register. Thus *cengkok*s for the *seleh* notes of *slendro* and *pelog* could be sketched in just a few lines. To give a rough idea, taking the *lik* of *Wilujeng*, where the *seleh* notes are either 1, 2 or 6, possible *suling cengkok*s for each one are:

Apart from the close similarity between them, it is clear that the notation can only make a vague attempt at indicating a possible rhythmic structure, through the proportional spacing, and any attempt to translate that into the staff notation used in the score would be too difficult to justify with confidence.

Perhaps the best way to understand the *suling* part (and also why the possibility of circular breathing is not exploited) is to imagine that, while the *rebab* imitates the human voice, the *suling* imitates a bird. Its wonderfully free and intermittent chirping does sound bird-like, and we should remember that song-birds are greatly loved by the Javanese.

Sindhen and *gerongan*

It was stated earlier that the most important vocal part in the gamelan, the *sindhen (-an)* (for solo female voice) is too complex, especially with regard to its rhythmic freedom, to be adequately notated in the cipher notation (as is the case with the *suling*). There are, however, notations of the *sindhenan* for complete pieces, and one may be offered for *Wilujeng*, with the caveat that it is a simple guide and not an exact representation of how it may be realized in performance. Other vocal interjections which often occur in gamelan music need not be considered for the purposes of the notation. They include the stylized shouts and ululations known as *senggakan* and *alok*. Their inclusion depends on the piece (they are not necessary in *Wilujeng*), the occasion and the mood. Usually they are performed by a small group of perhaps three or four men, whose main function is to sing the *gerongan*. This is a unison melody and is almost equal in importance to the *sindhenan*. Two features (apart from the sex of the performers) distinguish these vocal parts: the *gerongan* (which is metrically far more regular) is restricted to certain sections (usually the *lik*) of pieces, while the *sindhenan* tends to be more or less continuous throughout. Both, however, must fit the phrasing of the *balungan*, as well as the particular poetic metre on which they are based. In fact it is quite common to include the *gerongan* in Javanese cipher notations, so the *gerongan* of *Wilujeng*, sung only in the *lik*, has been easily incorporated into the score (allowing for a certain amount of extra ornamentation in performance). The text (*cakepan*) of both the *sindhen* and *gerongan* parts in the *lik* of *Wilujeng* is by Prince Mangkunegara IV (reigned 1853–81) and, typically of such texts, is somewhat obscure in meaning. A fairly literal rough English translation is given beneath the Javanese original:

1. *Parabe Sang Marabangun*
   His name is the noble Marabangun

   Sepat domba kali Oya
   A great fish in the river Oya

   Aja dolan lan wong priya
   Do not play games with men

   Nggerameh nora prasaja
   Appearances are deceptive

2. *Garwa Sang Sindura Prabu*
   The wife of the noble King Sindura

   Wicara mawa karana
   Speaks with a reason

   Aja dolan lan wanita
   Do not play games with women

   Tan nyata asring katarka
   Or you will attract slander

Unfortunately, such a translation does not capture a major feature of such texts, known as *wangsalan*, which can be translated as 'riddle', 'hint', or 'pun', but which is a complex and ingenious poetic system of resonance between certain words or phrases. The *dhalang* in a *wayang* often uses *wangsalan* to hint at the next piece he wants the gamelan to play, and it seems very characteristically Javanese to do things in what is both an imaginative and indirect way. Such a subtle use of language and cultural references only works in Javanese and a detailed analysis of the *wangsalan* in the above text would require more space and expertise than are available here. To give some idea, however, the clues are found in alternate lines. Thus we have to know that Marabangun also has the name Priya Wada, which obviously connects with the use of the word *priya* (man) in the third line, while the great fish in the second line would be, by inference, a carp, for which the word is similar to the *nggerameh* of the fourth line. The overt cautionary advice and moral instruction are fairly typical of Javanese song texts. This one is a particular favourite in Java, for exactly the same words, set to different *gerongan* and *sindhen* melodies, are used in several other pieces.

Kendhang

By now, the rather unsatisfactory word 'embellishment' to classify such a varied and important section of the gamelan has broken down. It certainly cannot be used to describe the function of the drums, which are something of an exception, not only because they are the only non-melodic instruments to play an important role in the ensemble, but also because their part is more akin to the foundation – rather than the decoration – of the musical edifice. Drum patterns are relatively standardized and easily notated. They are determined by the form of the piece, sometimes even by the tuning system. The drum pattern for *Wilujeng* is the standard one for the *ladrang* form. A *kendhang* player will learn the patterns for all the main forms, such as *lancaran*, *ketawang*, *ladrang*, and the larger *gendhing*s. When only the large *kendhang gendhing* (*kendhang ageng*), or that drum combined with the *kendhang ketipung* (as in *Ladrang Wilujeng*), are used, the parts are neither especially complex nor difficult to perform. When, however, the *ciblon* is introduced, or the drumming is to accompany dance or *wayang*, then an advanced knowledge and technique are required. The *ciblon* drum may be used in certain short pieces including some *ladrang*s, (though not *Wilujeng*), but it is more usually employed in large-scale pieces and in the slowest tempi, allowing the most elaborate patterns to be played. For the purposes of the score of *Wilujeng*, only the basic drum part for the *ladrang* form, played on the largest and smallest drum, indicated by the abbreviation '*kendhang II*' need be given. It must be remembered that the drummer is the nearest equivalent to a conductor. Signals to start and finish a piece, to make the transitions of tempo, dynamics, even tuning (where applicable) are usually given by the drums. The ending, called *suwuk*, is particularly important, and involves a special series of drum sounds. Without them the piece would not end but continue to repeat itself, or perhaps (from another drum signal) make a transition to another piece. An essential part of the *suwuk* is the gradual slowing down to the end of the piece. (A few pieces do the opposite and end by speeding up in a dramatic way, and this is known as *suwuk gropak*.) In most pieces (including *Wilujeng*) the final note is slightly delayed until after the stroke on the *gong ageng* (but this important performance convention is never shown in notation).

Perhaps the remarkable thing about the cueing function of the drums, which reflects the egalitarian and restrained nature of the gamelan, is that the drumming achieves this pre-eminence and yet remains unobtrusive (which is where any comparison with a conductor must end!). It is almost as if it is sensed rather than heard, and confirms what the rest of the gamelan already collectively feel. Loud, domineering drumming, unless for some special theatrical effect, is therefore not only unpleasant but unnecessary. The secret of the wonderful ensemble playing in gamelan music does not lie with just one instrument.

Provisional score of *Ladrang Wilujeng (lik)*

For a variety of reasons, discussed below, the qualification 'provisional' must be remembered in any mention of this score, the purpose of which is to provide a simple, representative extract of gamelan music, exemplifying the main points of this chapter. It should not be interpreted in the Western sense of the score as blue-print for any performance of the particular piece, but rather as one likely possibility among countless others of how the piece may be performed. A real analogy to the Western score in terms of gamelan music is in fact impossible, and, many would argue, undesirable, since it could lead to standardization and impoverishment. Just as no two gamelans should be tuned exactly alike, and should in general preserve a distinctive sound, so no two performances of the same piece should be identical or fixed through notation. Perhaps the best analogy between the present exercise and Western notation is with Baroque music, rather than with the more complete scores of the nineteenth and twentieth centuries. Just as a Baroque score may show only a melody and a bass with figures, so the usual gamelan notation (in the cipher system) is essentially a *balungan* and its colotomic support. The equivalents of the 'figures' are implied. They are added by knowledgeable musicians, according to their application of *garap*, and the results may vary greatly according to the skill of the musicians, just as in Baroque music. What we have here, to pursue the analogy, is a simple realization of the 'figures'. The composition could be performed as notated, but one would expect an expert group of performers to play a more complex version, and even a less advanced group would quickly explore new and varied possibilities.

Despite the many problems raised and the essential incompatibility with the ideals of gamelan performance, this attempt to make a score is of course neither futile nor even new. Kunst's thorough study includes a fragment of a score written by Javanese musicians in 1923[2] but, ironically, it relies on the usual unmodified staff notation, which has been eschewed in this book as too un-Javanese! This fascinating example apart, there is no real tradition of scores in gamelan music, so the layout here follows certain principles of Western scores alongside traditional gamelan groupings. Thus, in the centre is the *balungan* section (*peking*, *saron barung*, *demung*, and *slenthem*). Note that there are usually two *saron barung* (playing in unison). In this score they, and the *demung* and *slenthem*, carry the *balungan* in its simplest form. The slower *irama* (*irama dados*) means that the *peking* plays the *selang-seling* variation. Below the *balungan* instruments is the colotomic section (*kethuk-kempyang*, *kenong*, *kempul* and *gong ageng*), while above the *balungan* are the embellishing instruments. The leading melodic instrument, the *rebab*, is placed at the top of the score, and the leading rhythmic instruments, the *kendhangs* (two of them, as indicated by the

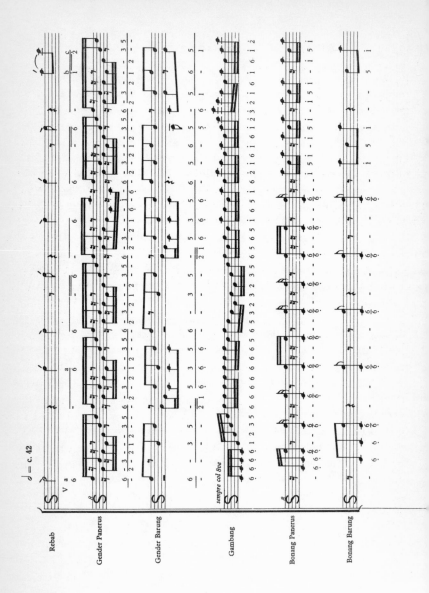

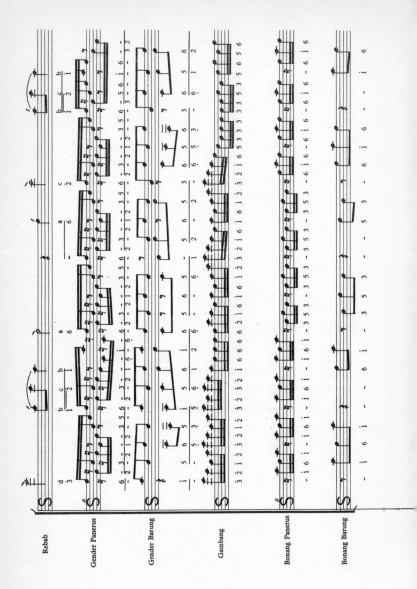

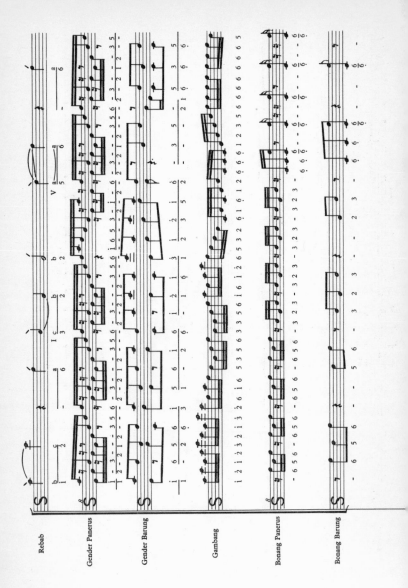

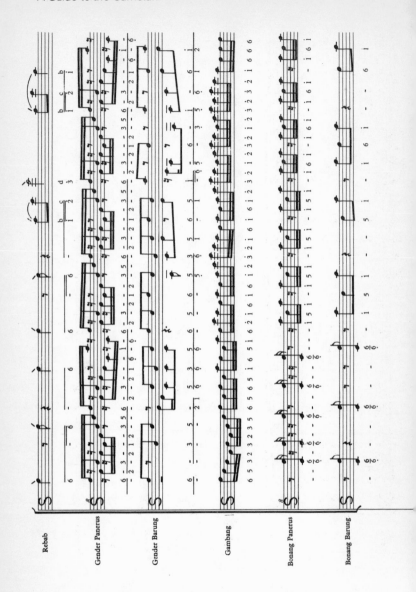

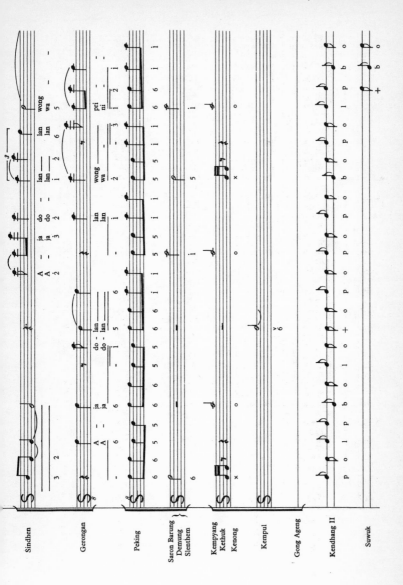

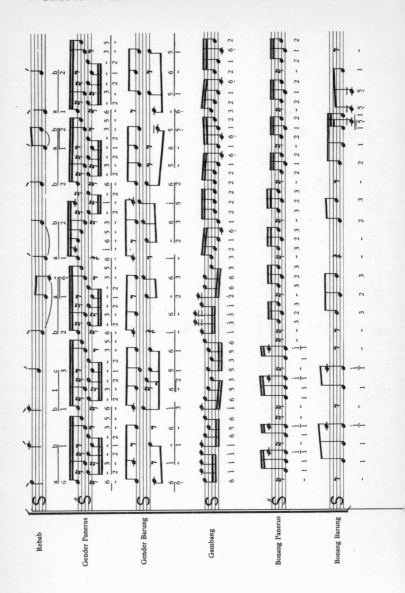

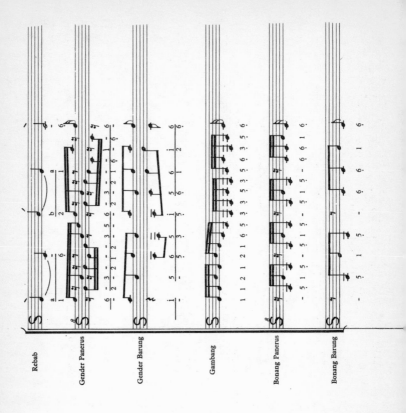

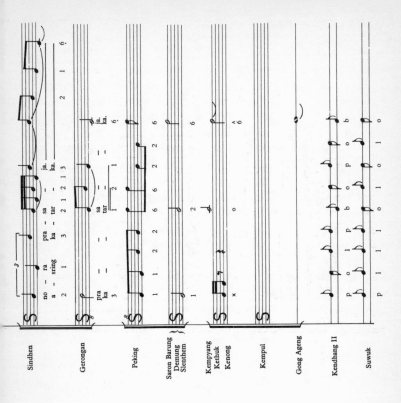

Roman numeral) are placed at the bottom. In general higher-pitched instruments are placed above lower-pitched ones.

Although the complete piece is in two sections, it was decided to give only the second section, the *lik*, in this score. For one thing, it is representative of the whole piece, thus obviating the need for pages of similar notation, and for another it is the section where all parts occur, including the *gerongan*. The *balungan* of the whole piece was given earlier (p. 80). A typical performance would begin with the *buka* (on *rebab*) leading into the first section (A), slowing down from *irama tanggung* to *irama dados*, going to the *lik* (B) and thereafter following an A–A–B form. The *lik* (given in the score) is therefore in *irama dados*, and two verses are given, assuming that the performance will follow a typical A–A–B–A–A–B form. The ending (*suwuk*) is at the end of the second time through the *lik* (B); thus there will be a ritardando to the final *gong*, (which is slightly delayed), and the last note (6) will be played just after the *gong*.

Finally, although the *slendro* version of *Wilujeng* is given, it is important to remember that it may also be performed in *pelog* (with some changes). The *slendro* version has been chosen because, of the two, it is generally regarded as the more important, and also because *slendro pathet manyura* is traditionally the tuning and *pathet* used for teaching beginners.

Notes

1 Kunst, op. cit., pp. 249–50.
2 Ibid., pp. 481–9.

Chapter 6

Conclusion

Although most of this book has concentrated on the music and instruments of the gamelan, we now return to the topic of the first chapter to consider why people outside Java are attracted to the gamelan, and want to study it seriously. These are still early days in the history of the gamelan in the West, and we may not yet have the necessary perspective. It is certainly not my intention in this book to play the missionary, preaching the salvation of the world's music through the gamelan. There are lessons in it for all of us, and, to paraphrase the well-known advertising slogan, it can reach those parts of our musical psyches that other musics leave untouched. But the popular Western idea that gamelan music is nothing less than a kind of mystical and secret rite is a misleading one. It has, of course, its spiritual aspects, and it is probably this quality that attracts people, in the same way that yoga and other manifestations of Hindu spiritualism have gained so many devout followers. Yet we should not forget that the Javanese have their bawdy side, and, like their Western counterparts, are susceptible to wine and women, and not only to song. It is, therefore, refreshing to read the work of healthy sceptics. James Siegel, who managed to produce a major study of life in the city of Solo with no more than a passing reference to the gamelan, wrote:

> Such orchestras are nearly always involved in quiet scandals. The female singer in particular is often engaged in intrigue with orchestra members. Her flirtations are likely to involve the whole of the orchestra.[1]

(This, no doubt, is the reason why more than one Westerner has been tempted to spend all his time playing in Javanese gamelans!) The

Javanese psyche remains complex and perhaps beyond our understanding. But we can gain insight through the music, and one thing the Javanese are not is rigidly purist. Westerners who prefer to believe the opposite are naive, failing to remember that one of the strengths of gamelan music is its propensity to reflect and absorb other influences. When the history of the gamelan in the West comes to be written, it may well provide a classic example of what anthropologists call 'marginal survival' whereby the centre of a culture constantly changes and evolves while its farthest-flung manifestations cling to traditional models, and even turn into museum cultures. A more optimistic analogy would be with dialects: every region has its own characteristics by which it is instantly recognizable, yet every variant form is still accepted and understood: *vive la différence*!

So much for speculation, but one thing we must believe is that the gamelan is here to stay. No doubt many see the gamelan only as a kind of delayed after-shock from the sixties (and some players encourage this view). But is there any such creature as the 'typical' gamelan player (remember we are discussing only the non-Javanese kind)? The cynic may say that the common bond is not so much a love for gamelan music, as failure in all others. Perhaps the most positive fact is that the gamelan attracts people from all walks of life, all social backgrounds, and all varieties of musical training, from rock musicians, to classically-trained artists, to (best of all) those whom our divisive culture would label 'non-musicians'. This variety of experiences and perceptions has its positive and negative aspects. At the sad end of the spectrum are those whose brief contact with the gamelan leads them to the simplistic conclusion that it is glorified child's play. The most frustrating character to argue with is the 'little European', for whom music consists exclusively of the great Germanic tradition. Pentatonicism and percussion are equated with childishness. Yet music is not a matter of *how many* notes are used, but *how* they are used. When first encountered, gamelan music may indeed seem simple. In reality it is a bottomless ocean: one can happily skim along its surface, but in reality its depths are profound, and even an expert Javanese musician cannot fathom them in a lifetime.

At the happy end of the spectrum are those for whom the child-like properties are among the music's most positive strengths. It is indeed bizarre that a middle-aged person, dressed in a business suit or some other formal attire, should be prepared to take off both shoes, sit on the floor, and hit a rather small percussion instrument; childhood memories will come flooding back, if only subconsciously. Such memories are just as likely to be painful as pleasurable, yet the possibility of reliving such experiences in a controlled and supportive situation through the gamelan must be one of the major factors contributing to the sense of well-being so many players experience. Nor should we overlook the element of controlled violence: in certain pieces many of the instruments must be struck hard. The context and aesthetic goal help focus this little release of aggression: it is harmless, but therapeutic.

One point which has always delighted me is that gamelan turns so many preconceptions about 'talent' and 'musicality' on their head. Perhaps this proves only that such notions are specific to our particular culture and should not be considered absolute or universal. Even so, this enthusiasm for 'other' musics represents an important step in breaking down outdated Western hegemonic dogma, and there is no doubt that the gamelan has been consciously adopted for this purpose by academics, notably in the ethnomusicology programs of colleges in the United States. Indeed, running a credible ethnomusicology program almost necessitates possessing a gamelan and we in the United Kingdom seem to be following the same path: the gamelan is, perhaps, something of a status symbol. It would be ironic, then, if pride and rivalry were stimulated by this music when, by its very nature, it avoids them. Competitiveness is the enemy; experienced and less experienced players contribute equally and help each other. The most welcome players are often those who have had no musical training, and even consider themselves 'unmusical'. The experience of playing gamelan is not guaranteed to prove them wrong, but, with effort and, above all, the right attitude, they can find that their contribution is no less valid than anyone else's. What the gamelan can do for them personally, outside the immediate context of playing in the ensemble, is another matter, but I can report small miracles, from cured headaches, to improved memory, to the most obvious benefit of just feeling happier and more confident.

Whether we should look for much more from gamelan playing is open to question. Whether to use it for financial gain, rather than as a strictly amateur activity in its best sense, raises questions of ethics, not to mention competence. The related issue of concert-giving is also open to debate, if only because the formality of the Western-style concert distorts the traditional function of the gamelan. The idea of playing gamelan music to a motionless and attentive audience, who are attending for that reason alone, and, who have, moreover, paid for it, is at variance with Javanese practice. Inevitably, the change of context will result in a change of music, and certainly in a change in the musicians. One of the most cherishable experiences of gamelan music in Java (recreated by some groups in the West) is the informal *klenengan*, where musicians get together to play, eat, drink and smoke, just for the enjoyment of it. People are welcome to come and listen, but their presence makes no difference. Western-style concerts can also be fun and exhilarating, and, above all else, they provide a goal for a group to work towards, but they can also foster a self-image that is mistaken, formal and self-important. We would do well to ask how the Javanese see us. There is no doubt that they are pleased at this interest in their culture, but they are among the most reserved and discreet people on earth and we cannot know what they are thinking. A walk down a street in Java will give some clues. The word pronounced 'londo' (foreigner) is frequently heard. Wearing batik shirts, smoking 'kretek' cigarettes and speaking a smattering of Indonesian will not disguise the fact that we are all 'londos' and can never be Javanese. However much we steep ourselves in Javanese culture, the mystery, and hence the power, remain intact.

Bearing these points in mind, we may conclude with two quotations about the power of the gamelan, the first from a Westerner involved with it as a performer and composer, and the second by a Javanese, who is not only an expert performer but the most experienced gamelan teacher in the West. Lou Harrison is characteristically pithy:

> Simply said, gamelan music is the most beautiful music in the world, and I for one see no reason to do any other kind of music ever again.[2]

This may not gain wide acceptance, especially among Europeans and composers who have not absorbed the style and found a language as confidently as Harrison. It should also be added that the study of gamelan music may reverse this inclination to eschew Western music, and actually enhance our appreciation not only of Debussy, Messiaen and Britten but also of Machaut, Josquin and Bach. Another analysis is, at least on the surface, easier to accept than Harrison's. It comes from the concluding 'personal notes' of a paper read at the 1986 Gamelan Festival in Vancouver by the Javanese Hardja Susilo:

I am sure that many of you have been asked why you are studying gamelan. Certainly it is not because the demand for gamelan players is so great. I believe it is a pleasant way to learn about another culture. It is another alternative to make music. It presents a different aesthetic experience. But to me the most interesting reason is the one that my fifth grade teacher gave us, namely that we should study gamelan and dance in order to refine our behavior. Goodness knows we needed it. I find it interesting in retrospect that we should study dance and music not to become the best dancers and musicians, but to become better persons. I suppose ultimately that is what counts. Playing gamelan will neither make me rich nor save my soul, but it might just make me a little more civilized.[3]

Yet even here the cynic may point out that it emphasizes the potential of gamelan music rather than what it may actually have achieved. Music should refine our behaviour and balance our emotions, but so should our behaviour and emotional control refine our music. The circle can only be broken by as much effort towards personal development as towards musical knowledge. I hope that this book will contribute to the latter, but the former is another story.

Notes

1 James T. Siegel; *Solo in the New Order: language and hierarchy in an Indonesian city* (Princeton University Press, 1986), p. 288.
2 Quoted in *Balungan*, Vol. II, No. 3, December 1986, p. 48.
3 Unpublished paper, distributed at the Vancouver festival, entitled 'Changing strategies for the cross-cultural krawitan experience: a quarter-century perspective', Honolulu, 22 May 1986.

Glossary

The policy is to provide as concise a definition as possible, according to how the term is used in this book, therefore without necessarily giving all meanings or etymologies.

alat bubut lathe used in gamelan manufacture to cut a groove on gongs
alok stylized male cry or shout
alus refined
awis (arang) widely-spaced (beats on the *kethuk*)
ayak-ayakan form of gamelan piece, especially associated with *wayang*

babon gamelan used as a model for the tuning of a new set
bahasa daérah regional language
Bahasa Indonesia official language of Indonesia
balungan skeletal melody of a gamelan composition, more correctly called *balunganing gendhing*. Different types include *balungan mlaku* (regular notes), *balungan ngadhal* (subdivided) and *balungan nibani* (alternating notes and rests)
barang name of note 7 in *pélog* and 1 in *sléndro* (see also *pathet*)
barang miring a tuning (also called *minir*) used in some *sléndro* pieces to impart a feeling of sadness through the use of certain notes between the fixed pitches, thereby restricting it to the voice and the *rebab*
bawa solo male vocal introduction to a gamelan piece
bedhaya court dance usually performed by nine women
bedhug large drum played with a mallet
bem name of note 1 in *pélog* (see also *pathet*)
bentuk (musical) form
berlian hard wood used to make *gambang wilah*
besalèn hut used for gamelan manufacture

bonang gong-chime, referring to the *bonang barung*. The *bonang pan-erus* is pitched an octave higher (see also *pencon*)

bremara small wooden sticks used to secure the supporting cord to the *wilah* of the *gendèr*s and *slenthem*

buka solo introductory phrase of a gamelan piece

bumbung tubular resonator (on the *gendèr*s and *slenthem*)

bunderan sphere, used in describing gongs

cakepan text (of vocal item)

cakilan toggle used to suspend gongs

celempung zither

cemengan black, unfiled condition of bronze

cèngkok melodic pattern used by embellishing instruments

ciblon see *kendhang*

demung gamelan instrument (see also *saron* and *wilah polos*)

dhalang puppeteer

embat intervallic structure

entol long pole used, in conjuction with the shorter *umbul*, in gamelan manufacture

gadhon chamber gamelan of the softer instruments (see also *soran*)

gambang xylophone, usually referring to the wooden type (*gambang kayu*). There is also the obsolete bronze type (*gambang gangsa*)

gamelan generic term for ensemble of predominantly struck instruments found in the Indonesian region, especially in Java and Bali. The different types are usually distinguished by suffixes, for example the Balinese *gong gedhé* (large, archaic gamelan), *gong kebyar* (modern version), *gamelan angklung*, and *gamelan bebonangan* (ensembles carried in processions). Javanese gamelans are often given names, for example Gamelan Kyai Kanyut Mèsem (in Solo) and Gamelan Sekar Pethak (in York). A set in one of the two tuning systems is termed a *gamelan sepangkon*, and in both a *gamelan seprangkat*

gangsa bronze used in gamelan manufacture. Can also be used as an alternative word for gamelan

garap the way by which musicians work out their parts in a composition

gatra unit of four notes, rests, or combination of both

gembyang octave. Also used for the octave playing style on the *bonangs gendèr* gamelan instrument, referring to the *gendèr barung*. The *gendèr panerus* is pitched an octave higher (see also *wilah blimbingan*). The accompanying quartet of *gendèr*s in the Balinese shadow play is called *gendèr wayang*

gendhing generic term for a gamelan composition, also used in the title of larger pieces, for example *Gendhing Babar Layar*. Such large pieces are also classified according to the leading melodic instrument and are mostly *gendhing rebab*, with a sizeable minority of *gendhing bonang*. Suffixes, such as *klenèngan* (concert), *beksan* (dance), *wayangan* (shadow play), *pakurmatan* (ceremonial), *gecul* (funny), *gobyog* (cheerful) and *tlutur* or *welasan* (sad) may be used to classify pieces according to mood and usage

gérongan male chorus

gong this is used in two ways in this book: (1) as the general organological term for the shape of many instruments found in the gamelan (see *pencon*); (2) as the Javanese use it, specifically to refer to the main gong of the gamelan: the *gong ageng*, or its smaller substitute *gong suwukan*. To distinguish, this latter usage is italicized

gongan section of music between strokes on the *gong*

gong kemodhong instrument normally found in reduced ensembles as a substitute for the large *gong* (see also *wilah pencon*)

iklas detachment, repose

imbal interlocking patterns of alternate notes on two similar instruments

inggah second main section of a large *gendhing*

irama related to tempo, but strictly a concept of rhythmic proportions between instrumental parts. The different *irama*s are called *irama lancar* (also a faster version called *irama gropak*), *irama tanggung*, *irama dados* (or *dadi*), *irama wiled* (or *wilet*), and *irama rangkep*

iringan accompaniment

jati teak

kacapi zither from Sunda (West Java)

karawitan gamelan music (specifically instrumental and/or vocal music in the Javanese tuning systems) *kawi* archaic form of Javanese, still used in *wayang* and certain other connections with gamelan

kebyar originally a dance, and then the prevalent style of gamelan music in Bali this century (see also *gamelan*)

kecak Balinese male chorus consisting of interlocking shouts mainly of the syllable *cak*

kecèr small cymbals often used in the gamelan

kemanak a pair of bronze banana-shaped instruments often used in specific vocal choruses

kempel denotes a clear, focused sound from a newly made gong

kempul smaller hanging gong (see also *pencon*)

kempyang see *kethuk*

kendhang drums of the gamelan, called (from largest to smallest) *kendhang gendhing* (or *ageng*), *kendhang wayangan*, *kendhang batangan*, or *kendhang ciblon* (or simply *ciblon*), and *kendhang ketipung* (or simply *ketipung*)

kenong largest of the gongs supported from beneath (see also *pencon*)

kenongan section of music between strokes on the *kenong*

kepatihan the cipher system of notation generally used for gamelan music

keplok rhythmic, interlocking clapping, usually associated with *ciblon* drumming

keprak small wood block drum

kepyak bronze plates struck by the *dhalang*

kerep closely spaced (beats on the *kethuk*)

ketawang form of gamelan piece with 16 beats to the *gongan* (for example *Ketawang Puspawarna*)

ketawang gendhing larger-scale form

keteg pulse or beat, one quarter of a *gatra*

kethuk small gong, suspended from beneath, with which the *kempyang* forms a pair (see also *pencon*)

kikir file used in gamelan manufacture. Many are used, ranging from the coarse *kikir patar*, to the blade *kikir kesik*

kinthilan interlocking pattern between two *saron*s, used especially in *wayang*

klenèngan concert music, i.e. gamelan music not used as accompaniment

kowi cup used for molten bronze in gamelan manufacture

krama High Javanese

kraton court or palace

kuthuk kuning gembyang name of a *cèngkok*

ladrang form of gamelan piece with 32 beats to the *gongan* (for example *Ladrang Wilujeng*)

lagu melody

lakon story of a *wayang* play

lamus bellows to activate the fire used for gamelan manufacture

lancaran form of gamelan piece with 16 beats to the *gongan* (but with a different structure from *ketawang*), For example *Lancaran Ricik-ricik* and *Lancaran Tropongbang*

laras tuning system, of which there are two (see *pélog* and *sléndro*)

laya tempo

lik usually the second section of a gamelan piece, characterized by a higher tessitura and a *gérongan* chorus

lima name of note 5 in both *pélog* and *sléndro* (see also *pathet*)

manyura see *pathet*

mérong first main section of a large *gendhing*

minggah used in the title of a large *gendhing* to indicate the main structural changes in the transition from *mérong* to *inggah*

minir see *barang miring*

mipil embellishing pattern on the *bonang*s. According to the *irama* it can be slow (*mipil lamba*) or doubled (*mipil rangkep*). Also called *pipilan*

nem name of note 6 in both *pélog* and *sléndro* (see also *pathet*)

ngelik full name for *lik*

ngencot technique of striking a *wilah* at the same time as damping it

niyaga gamelan player

nyacah variations played on the *saron* and *peking* in pieces like *srepegan* and *sampak* during a *wayang* performance

ompak usually denotes the transition between the *mérong* and *inggah* of a large *gendhing*, but is sometimes also used to refer to the first section of a shorter form, such as a *ladrang* (often written as *umpak*)

padhang-ulihan antecedent and consequent. Two words used to describe the phrase-structure of gamelan pieces

Pak shorter form of Bapak, used to address an older man. Roughly equivalent to 'Mr'

palu hammer used in gamelan manufacture

panji the name of a Javanese prince, borrowed for the major role in gamelan manufacture

pathet sub-modalities within each of the two *laras*. The three *pathet*s of *sléndro* are called *pathet nem*, *pathet sanga* and *pathet manyura*, and the three of *pélog* are called *pathet lima*, *pathet nem* and *pathet barang*. A fourth, rarer, *pathet* in *pélog* is called *pathet manyura* or *nyamat*, and sometimes a combination of *pathet*s *lima* and *nem* (in *pélog*) is called *pathet bem*

pathetan sung by the *dhalang* in a *wayang*, with reduced instrumental accompaniment, or played just by those instruments as preludes or postludes to gamelan pieces, of which the primary function is to establish or confirm the *pathet*

peking nickname, generally used in this book, for the *saron panerus*, which is the highest-pitched instrument of its group (an octave above the *saron barung*. See also *wilah polos*)

pelamus bellows operator

pelandhan water bath used in gamelan manufacture

pélog one of the two *laras*, comprising seven notes

pencon gong, applied generally to circular instruments with a central boss (the part which is struck). Of the many examples and sizes in the gamelan, two main shapes may be discerned. In the Javanese terminology they are strictly defined by the way in which they are supported: *pencon gandhul*, hanging, and *pencon pangkon*, supported from beneath. All *pencon gandhul* are of a flatter shape (for example the *gong ageng*, *gong suwukan* and *kempul*) and most *pencon pangkon* have more raised sides (for example the *kenong*). Some instruments, notably the *bonang*s, and *kethuk-kempyang* pair mix these shapes, but their gongs are all supported from beneath

pencu central boss of a gong

pendhapa palace audience hall, or kind of pavilion, which usually houses at least one gamelan

penengah one of group who hammer during gamelan manufacture *penépong* another in the group who hammer

pengalap man who carries the metal from the fire to the anvil during gamelan manufacture

pengapit another in the group who hammer

pengarep another in the group who hammer

pengider man who turns the metal on the anvil during gamelan manufacture

penyingèn mould used in gamelan manufacture

perunggu Indonesian word for bronze

pesindhèn woman who sings the *sindhèn*

pinjalan interlocking pattern between the *slenthem* and *demung*, combined with a different pattern on the *saron*s

pipilan (see *mipil*)

plèsèdan the anticipation by an instrument, for example *kenong*, of a strong (usually repeated) note

prapèn charcoal fire used in gamelan manufacture

rāga melodic basis of Indian classical music

rancak wooden rack, frame or case used to support the bronze parts of gamelan instruments

rasa roughly synonymous with mood or feeling, originating in Indian aesthetic theory

rebab two-stringed fiddle

rejasa tin

ricik tool (referring in this book to those used in gamelan manufacture), also the instruments themselves

sampak form of gamelan piece, especially associated with *wayang*

sanga see *pathet* and *saron*

sanggan a kind of hook used to support the connecting cord between the *wilah* on the *slenthem* and *gendèr*s

saron gamelan instrument, referring to the *saron barung*. The *saron panerus* (commonly known as *peking*) is pitched an octave higher, and the *saron demung* (commonly known just as *demung*) is pitched an octave lower (see also *wilah polos*). Although the number of *wilah* on the *saron* is usually seven, a special one with nine keys in the *sléndro* tuning is sometimes found for use in *wayang*, and is called *saron wayang* or *saron (wilah) sanga*

sedheng medium (referring to tempo)

sekaran florid cadential phrase

selang-seling pattern, based on pairs of notes, played on the *peking*

sèlèh note of resolution or focus on which parts tend to meet, usually the last note of a *gatra*

senggakan stylized interjections sung by men

serimpi court dance usually performed by four women

seseg fast (tempo)

sindhèn (-an) ornate and prominent vocal line in a gamelan piece sung by a solo female. It can also refer to the unison male and female chorus sung in the accompaniment to the court dances *bedhaya* and *serimpi*

siter small zither

sléndro one of the two *laras*, comprising five notes

slenthem gamelan instrument (see also *wilah blimbingan*)

soran loud, usually referring to instruments like the *saron* family and *bonang*s, and excluding the softer instruments at the front of the gamelan. In effect the opposite of *gadhon*

srepegan form of gamelan piece, especially associated with *wayang*

suling end-blown bamboo flute

suluk chants sung by the *dhalang* in a *wayang*

suwuk ending of a piece, usually by slowing down. If the opposite (speeding up) it is called *suwuk gropak*

suwukan see *gong*

tabuh mallet, used to strike gamelan instruments

talu overture to a *wayang*

tamban slow (tempo)

tandhes sunken anvil, used in gamelan manufacture

tari dance

tembaga copper

tikel groove around the central boss on gongs

tumbuk exchange note on which the two *laras* coincide

ulihan see *padhang-ulihan*

umbul see *entol*

umpak see *ompak*

wangsalan riddle or other word-play featured in Javanese texts *wayang* refers to the shadow puppet play *wayang kulit*. Other forms of *wayang* are known by their full name, for example *wayang wong* or *wayang orang* in which actors and actresses are used instead of puppets

wela omission of a colotomic part, usually just after a stroke on the *gong*

wilah bar or plate of a gamelan instrument. Apart from those of the *gambang*, they are all bronze (or other metal) and two types may be distinguished: (1) the thick bar with a smooth curved surface, called *wilah polos* or *lugas* (used on the instruments of the *saron* family); (2) the thin rectangular plate with a ribbed surface called *wilah blimbingan* (used on the *gendèr*s and *slenthem*). A third type, called *wilah pencon*, has a boss in the middle, but is not used in the typical modern bronze gamelan, except for the optional *gong kemodhong*

Further Reading

Many scholarly writings on the subject of *karawitan* have been published, especially in American journals of ethnomusicology, Asian music, and Indonesian studies. The aim here, however, is to suggest a few more generally available books which will draw the reader into the subject. In the list below, 1, 2, 4, 5, 6 and 8 are all substantial works of scholarly dimensions. Number 8, still a classic, is included for those who wish to find out more about the Balinese types of gamelan. 7, 9, and 10 are shorter introductions to aspects of the subject touched upon in this book, while number 3 is a journal devoted to the world of gamelan for those who may wish to subscribe.

1. Becker, Judith, *Traditional Music in Modern Java*, University Press of Hawaii, 1980
2. Becker, Judith and Alan H. Feinstein, eds., *Karawitan: Source Readings in Javanese Gamelan and Vocal Music*, 3 vols, University of Michigan, 1984, 1987, 1988
3. Diamond, Jody, ed., *Balungan*, a publication of the American Gamelan Institute, Box 9911, Oakland, California 94613
4. Hood, Mantle, *The Evolution of Javanese Gamelan*, 3 vols, Heinrichshofen, 1980, 1984, 1988
5. 'Indonesia', in Stanley Sadie, ed., *The New Grove Dictionary of Music and Musicians*, Macmillan, 1980, Vol. IX, pp. 167–220
6. Kunst, Jaap, *Music in Java*, 2 vols, Martinus Nijhoff, 1973
7. Lindsay, Jennifer, *Javanese Gamelan*, Oxford University Press, 1979
8. McPhee, Colin, *Music in Bali*, Yale University Press, 1966
9. van Ness, Edward C. and Shita Prawirohardjo, *Javanese Wayang Kulit: an Introduction*, Oxford University Press, 1980
10. Vulliamy, Graham and Ed Lee, eds., *Pop, Rock and Ethnic Music in School*, Cambridge University Press, 1982

Suggestions for listening

This list is by no means exhaustive, and represents only some of the LP recordings of gamelan music which have appeared in Europe and the United States. The large Indonesian cassette industry is not included because its products, covering just about everything mentioned in this book, are not generally obtainable in the West. Apart from reasonable availability, the main criteria are quality and interest. A very good place to start (and probably the best value for money) is the Nonesuch Explorer Series (USA), which has fine LPs of Central Javanese and Balinese gamelans. If a recording in the list is deleted or otherwise hard to find in the shops, it can often be found in good record libraries.

Central Java

Javanese Court Gamelan, three records: Nonesuch Explorer Series, H-72044, H-72074, and H-72083
Indonesia 1: Java Court Music, Unesco Collection: a Musical Anthology of the Orient, 31, Bärenreiter-Musicaphon BM 30 SL 2031
Java: l'art du Gamelan Musiques de l'Asie traditionnelle, vol. 7, Playa Sound PS 33507
– the best and most relevant recordings for this book (although the majority represent the Jogjanese traditions).
Java: Gamelans from the Sultan's Palace in Jogjakarta 'Musical Traditions in Asia', double album, Archiv 2723 017
– a selection of archaic ceremonial gamelans, and a whole side devoted to a modern standard. The contents reappear on other records, but it is worth looking out for this complete original.

Street music of Central Java Lyrichord LLST 7310
    – a folk perspective on gamelan music, as it is played by wandering street ensembles in Jogja, with an emphasis on portable instruments (zither and drum) and voices.

Surinam: Javanese music Lyrichord LLST 7317
    – a glimpse of a culture transplanted thousands of miles away from its source, by a Javanese community in South America.

The other areas (West Java and Bali) are not covered in this book, but a few representative recordings are included for general interest, and sheer enjoyment:

West Java

Sunda: les kratons de Cirebon Collection Musique du Monde 2, Galloway records GB 600 521
    – Cirebon is both geographically and stylistically on the border between West and Central Java and another point of interest is that it supplied the gamelan with which Debussy may have been most familiar.

Sunda: le gamelan degung Collection Musique du Monde 5, Galloway records GB 600 524
    – a typical and popular modern ensemble, beautifully exemplifying the characteristics of Sundanese music.

Bali

Among the wealth of recordings available, my suggestions are all from the Nonesuch Explorer Series:

Music from the Morning of the World H-72015
    – Pandit Nehru's description of Bali makes a wonderful title for this taster miscellany of Balinese music.

Golden Rain H-72028
    – More extended examples of the most famous Balinese music: the *gong kebyar* and the *kecak* chorus.

Music for the Balinese shadow play H-72037
   – pieces by the *gender wayang* ensemble, though not in the context of an actual *wayang* performance.

Gamelan Semar Pegulingan H-72046
   – the ensemble of the Balinese love god, with appropriate music of ravishing beauty.

Gamelan in the New World

Gamelan in the New World. Two records by Gamelan Son of Lion (New York), Folkways Records FTS 31312 and FTS 31313
   – another idea of a displaced culture, but this time to North America, and the instruments, musicians and compositions are all Western. A modern phenomenon worthy of note, even if many would claim that this is not really gamelan. Its inspiration certainly is.

Among the many recordings of Lou Harrison's music, three discs (all produced in the USA) which include his special gamelans, may be suggested:

Double Concerto for Violin and Cello with Javanese Gamelan TR
   Records TRC 109

La Koro Sutro New Albion Records NA 015 (issued on CD)

Main Bersama-Sama, Threnody for Carlos Chavez, and Serenade Composers Recordings, Inc. CRI SD 455

Index